35°

*Life with
the painters
of
La Ruche*

Life With the Painters of La Ruche

Marevna

Macmillan Publishing Co., Inc.
NEW YORK

Macmillan Publishing Co., Inc.
866 Third Avenue, New York, N.Y. 10022

Library of Congress Catalog Card Number: 73–10564

First American Edition 1974

Extracts from *Life in Two Worlds* reproduced by kind
permission of Abelard Schumann

Translation from the original Russian by Natalia Heseltine

The author and publishers would also like to thank
Oscar Ghez, Director of the Modern Art Foundation,
Geneva, for his great help and the generous loan of
illustrative material.

Printed in the United States of America

Contents

List of Illustrations vii

Preface by Robert L. Herbert ix

I   Paris 1912-1914: the Café Rotonde and the
painters of La Ruche 3

II   Diego and Marevna 55

III   Soutine: an appreciation 143

Epilogue 199

Index 208

Illustrations

between pages 86 and 87

1   Michel Kikoine Self portrait (The Wounded Hunter), 1929
    Modern Art Foundation, Geneva. Photo Raymond Asseo

2   Marevna Portrait of Kisling
    Modern Art Foundation, Geneva

3   Mané Katz Wandering musicians, 1927
    Modern Art Foundation, Geneva

4   Marevna Portrait of Mané Katz
    Modern Art Foundation, Geneva

5   Marevna Homage to Diaghilev and to the friends of the
    Train Bleu
    Modern Art Foundation, Geneva

6   Marevna Homage to the friends of Montparnasse
    Modern Art Foundation, Geneva

7   Marevna Two women weeping, 1954
    Modern Art Foundation, Geneva

8 **Diego M. Rivera** Portrait of the Dutch sculptor, Fisher
   The author. Photo John Webb, Brompton Studio

9 **Marevna** Green landscape
   Modern Art Foundation, Geneva
   Old Provençal peasant man
   Modern Art Foundation, Geneva
   Old Provençal peasant woman
   Michael Rubinstein. Photo James Daubeney

10 **Marevna** Marika nude with Persian rug, 1946
   The author

11 **Chaim Soutine** Carcass of an ox, 1923
   Modern Art Foundation, Geneva

12 **Marevna** Portrait of Soutine
   Modern Art Foundation, Geneva

13 **Chaim Soutine** Woman bathing, *c.* 1927
   Monsieur and Madame Marcellin Castaing
   Photo Arts Council of Great Britain
   Chaim Soutine
   Windy Day, Auxerre, 1939
   The Phillips Collection, Washington, D.C.
   Photo Arts Council of Great Britain

14 **Chaim Soutine** House at Oisème, 1934
   Richard H. Emerson
   Photo Arts Council of Great Britain

15 **Chaim Soutine** Hanging turkey, *c.* 1926
   Collection: Richard S. Zeisler, New York, N.Y.
   Photo Arts Council of Great Britain

16 **Marc Chagall** En route (Wandering Jew)
   Modern Art Foundation, Geneva

Original line drawings by Marevna

Preface

For those privileged to know her, Marevna exhibits undiminished those qualities which explain something of her painting and her writing. She flatters her companions by responding to their interests, for she has always looked upon other persons, as upon the slightest physical events (say, the color of an umbrella or the distinguishing gait of a friend) as part of the dialogue with life which she has always maintained. Despite long periods of poverty and isolation, and despite a relative innocence of the main currents of twentieth-century art, she has never been alone. She has always looked actively, that is, consciously, upon all that she sees, never taking it for granted, but applying a sense of meaning in order to comprehend it. Like the most idealistic members of today's communes of young people (who would understand her instinctively) she finds in all features of her environment a value we should call 'spiritual' in the broad sense of 'non-material.'

It is perhaps because she has been a nomad—from Russia to France to Holland to England—that Marevna has always found in people the permanence of values which geography denied her. Her best paintings exhibit the personal qualities of other nomads, such as the *Little Negro Girl* of 1938, or *The Malagasy Woman* of 1942, both painted in Cannes, that nomad's port. (Her and Diego Rivera's daughter, Marika, was her favorite model in the 1930s, and she too was a modern nomad.)

Marevna's painting, although widely scattered and seldom

reproduced, was at its most interesting from about 1928 to 1942. She had come to Paris in the heyday of Cubism, in 1912, and her first mature work was a form of figurative Cubism. Her own distinctive style was formed by the late 1920s, a belated Neo-Impressionism in which the paint or watercolor was applied in small, rather separate strokes. These follow an instinctive system of value gradation and tend toward the grey middle tones, and therefore do not constitute the mixture of intense hues associated with Seurat, Signac, and the original Neo-Impressionists. The integrity of her style was championed from 1928 to 1935 by Gustave Kahn, the Symbolist friend of Seurat and Signac who was still a vigorous critic in his later years. He apparently saw in her work this naïve and direct blend of hieratic style and tangible life-qualities which is so surprising. The explanation perhaps lies in Marevna's partial isolation, brought about by real poverty. It spared her the constant comparisons with the shifting tide of modern art which could have made her self-conscious about her style. This same innocence shows in her judgments of artists' work, from Leonardo to Soutine, but there is little naïveté in her judgment of people. Zadkine and Ehrenburg, Modigliani and Rivera are recorded with an intensity and a frankness that show how Marevna understood character by way of its exterior manifestations, rather the way a good playwright absorbs dialogue as the exhibition of inward meaning. In the memories of Marevna we have something of the youth of our century as it lives in the heart of a very young old wanderer.

New Haven, Conn. Robert L. Herbert

1
Paris 1912–1914: the Café Rotonde and the painters of La Ruche

Paris 1912–1914:
the Café Rotonde
and the painters
of La Ruche

The train was running into Paris, the capital of the world. My expectation mounted as we passed the fortifications in the suburbs and the little wooden huts encircled by tiny kitchen gardens. At last the first Paris buildings appeared. Old ones, their walls blackened by smoke from the trains and pasted over with advertisements in colour inviting me to drink *du bon* Dubonnet, Curaçao and Martini, and then, further on, suggesting that I take Vittel for the kidneys and Vichy for the liver. Javel bleaching fluid offered me linen whiter than that spread on balconies to dry amid black, smelly dust. Through the windows of the houses one could see pale, desperate looking housewives making beds, shaking out dubiously clean sheets and blankets and faded carpets. Was this Paris? The Paris of my dreams? I recalled the overwhelming excitement of my arrival in Moscow and later in Rome. Those two cities had given me a different welcome. Moscow had glittered under the gold of innumerable cupolas, and the intoxicating sound of the bells had made me dizzy; the Kremlin had looked like a fairy tale castle, drawing me towards it, conquered and quivering. In Rome, with its resplendent, violent sunlight, I had been stirred by the ancient buildings surrounded with green hills, by the imposing, majestic St Peter's that contained, I knew, a thousand and one treasures within its walls, by the strangeness, the noises, the smells that only an Italian town can release.

But my disappointment with Paris vanished as soon as I left

the Gare de Lyon and penetrated further into that disturbing, alluring city. Borne off in a cab by the Russian friends of Capri with whom I was going to stay, I looked from right to left, left to right, eager not to miss a thing. It was the autumn of 1912. I was twenty years old.

The streets swarmed with people. Newspaper vendors ran shouting the headlines in *Paris-Soir*, *L'Intran*, etc., or stood at street corners or in kiosks covered with brilliantly coloured posters advertising shows to suit every taste. Women with barrows sold flowers or vegetables; fishwives cried their wares in hoarse southern voices. They were a curious, gay spectacle, these walking markets—the 'Four Seasons'. The market women wore short, pleated skirts that showed rounded knees and firm calves sheathed in black woollen stockings, and black wooden shoes with red heels. Their shoulders were covered with the *caraco*, a knitted jacket with the neck high at the back. They wore the most improbable hats and sometimes, when their hair was arranged and pomaded in the Spanish style, they had almost the look of saucy *cocottes*.

I took in everything avidly. Chestnuts were being roasted in the open air, and the appetizing smell made my mouth water. Fried potatoes were on sale too, cooked on portable stoves and served with hot, little pink sausages. In days to come I was often to treat myself to these dishes of the people, delicious but, alas, fearfully indigestible. I saw countless cabs drawn by panting horses, who hobbled painfully as they dragged their heavy loads; they were continually being passed by brazen red taxis, which I did not like nearly so well. Heavy drays loaded with sacks of coal and wood for the coming winter caused spectacular traffic blocks. I could see that on foot one risked being crushed unceremoniously by one of the omnibuses drawn by huge, restive horses or by one of the electric trams or one of those famous red taxis. Crossing a main road in Paris in those days was a real adventure.

I observed, here and there on the boulevards, queer iron screens carrying advertisements for Chocolat Menier. Men partly disappeared behind the screens, all that remained visible of them their straddled feet and their heads under bowler hats and caps

4

and turbans and the occasional *calotte* of a priest. The sight was so odd that I could not help laughing. I asked for an explanation of these extraordinary looking erections.

'Why, those are the *vespasiennes*, Marie Marevna. The pride of Paris.'

I had seen nothing like them in Moscow, Tiflis, or even Rome. In those cities men of all classes urinated against walls, trees and gates. In Rome, well-dressed ladies would stop in the middle of the street, raise their skirts and relieve themselves, taking no notice of passers-by, who took no notice of them. I myself, during long walks about the eternal city, used to take cover in deserted yards or behind half-built houses; I found this natural. My friends informed me that things were different in Paris. There were Chocolats Menier for women too, but these were near the stations and on the main boulevards, and so the usual recourse was to order something in a café that had a W.C. for the use of its customers.

My Russian friends lived in a small, modest establishment. I stayed with them for three weeks, and then they found me two rooms on the fourth floor of a building in the rue Méchain, beside the boulevard de la Santé. One room I used as a dressing room and box room, keeping canvases, frames and suitcases there. The room I lived and worked in was pleasant and intimate. I furnished it simply. There was a narrow sofa, a chair, an armchair big enough to sleep in, two Caucasian carpets in warm colours and cushions everywhere. There was a little Turkish table for the tea that was always ready, a work table with a shaded lamp and some what-nots to hold my books and my drawing paper. A looking-glass hung on one wall and my canvases on the others. Incense smouldered in a burner, redolent with the smell of my beloved East.

Only the boulevard de la Santé and the pretty little garden of the house separated me from the famous Santé prison. The high, grey, gloomy walls and the little cell windows, securely barred, made a striking contrast to the fine, blossoming chestnuts and the gay shrubs in the garden where, in spring and summer, from morning to night, blackbirds whistled. Sometimes I would lean

5

my elbows on the windowsill, watching the coming of night with its soft shades of blue, pink and mauve in the shadows. Little by little the trees lost their green colour, changed into a mass of reddish brown, finally became dark. The misty sky cleared here and there, and stars winked mysteriously at me. How hard and cold the lights of the prison seemed beside all this. As I breathed in the fresh, balmy scent of the garden, I felt very happy compared with the unfortunates locked in behind the walls opposite.

No noise reached as high as the fourth floor, and sometimes the silence was so profound that I wondered whether there really were any human beings in the prison after all.

* * *

Every artist dreams of an absolutely free life and freedom to create. He wants to travel, to see and paint landscapes and objects that please him and faces and figures of people who attract him. But the awareness with which he is born is often smothered by the weight of distorted forms, imposed on him by inheritance or treatment received in childhood, in which he fails to recognize himself and by which he is imprisoned for a time. Only later will he learn that the landscapes, objects, faces and figures of his creative work have emerged from his childhood memories.

It was in Paris I was to meet Soutine, who is to me the greatest painter of the Paris milieu in which I lived and worked, and to whom I will return in detail later. My friendship with him was based not only on the strong interests and close friends we had in common, but also on certain childhood influences. Although we grew up very differently indeed, we shared a profound uncertainty in our early years, along with a passionate love of the nature and folklore of the vast expanses of Russia. The delight in the artistic liberation Paris gave us was slightly ambiguous, for we were left with a deep nostalgia for the forests, plains and rivers of our native land.

When I think about my childhood, I seem to smell again the wild scents of the steppes—damp wood on the banks of the Volga

6

and Kazanka rivers, the fragrance of the boundless forest, dead leaves, autumn. I was born in a village near Cheboksary, then a small provincial town in the Kazan District, now the capital of the Chuvash Socialist Republic. I never knew my mother, as Soutine knew his. I only know that she left when I was little and gave me to my father because she was so poor. My sister, who was three years older than me, stayed with her. My brother being a weakling died as a baby. It is an unhappy thing for a child to grow up without a mother, especially a little girl.

The people I remember best are my father, Bronislav Vikientievich Stebelsky, a Polish aristocrat and a forestry official in the Tsar's service, and my old nurse Nyanyushka in her black cotton dress and white kerchief, who washed and dressed me and brushed my hair, fed me and told me wonderful, fantastic stories when I was in bed. My father was often away from home, seeing to it that the Tartars, Cheremiss and Chuvash did not chop down trees without permission or kill too much game. When I was old enough, Father mounted me on a horse, and we would ride off to a marvellous hut in the woods where he kept cases of coloured butterflies, beetles, caterpillars and other insects, many of them harmful to the forest. He would tell me all about the forest and its animal and bird life, but I preferred my nurse's stories, which opened up a whole private world of visions for me.

My father was a great huntsman, and I enjoyed his happy expression, the animated faces of the other huntsmen and the shouts of the Tartars as they drove in deer, hares and foxes on their shaggy little horses. But my heart was with the animals and I was happy when they escaped.

Sometimes my father, coming back late from the hunt and looking like Jack Frost with snow clinging to his enormous greatcoat, his fur hat, his tobacco-stained moustache and his eyebrows, would toss a dead hare or a dead quail on my bed and say, 'Here you are. The forest has sent you a gift.'

I would cover the blood-stained, motionless creature with my blanket and press it close to me, willing it to come to life again. At such times my father appeared terrible to me, and I longed to run

7

off to Nyanyushka so that she could cradle me in her arms and tell me a story to comfort me.

But my father feared the effects of the nurse's fantastic stories and sent her away. For the most part, I was left to grow up in our huge house with just the cook, the maid and the coachman. My father did not like cats and he was merciless to his five dogs. I often cried with loneliness.

My father was a strange and violent man. He disciplined his dogs and his servants and a young secretary—with a solid *knout* which he kept in a conspicuous position near the door. One day he said to me in a serious tone: 'If you are too wicked, I'll punish you with it!' At that moment I remembered I was alone with my father. My nurse had gone and I had neither nurse nor governess; as a result I gave him a lot of trouble trying to make me behave. I replied, 'If you do that—I'll run to the forest and never come back.' Papa ruffled my short hair and said with a smile, 'No, you know that I would never hit you.' And it was true he never touched me, he would just make huge eyes at me, which I didn't much like.

On winter evenings, Father sometimes made fascinating fretwork boxes with figures of devils and birds. I would ask him innumerable questions, for I longed to learn everything I could.

But he would say with a smile, 'When you grow older, you'll learn everything. For now, clean my gun and make up some cartridges. I want you to be an eaglet, not a chick. Understand?'

'Yes, I understand,' I would reply gravely, and set to work filling cartridge cases with powder and shot.

We would have our evening meal of *kasha* with milk and butter in the kitchen. As a little girl, I was sick from eating too much hot bread (which was made at home once a week) or food which was too indigestible for a child and which eventually made me quite seriously ill. Outside was the silence of the winter night; inside, the dogs sleeping under the kitchen table and my father's eyes shining like those of a kindly spirit of the woods. At such times my father was very dear and close to me. He would stroke my hair and I would fall asleep in his lap, dreaming of the forest, of Baba-

8

Yaga, of the White Wolf and Sister Fox, of bears . . .

Perhaps he sensed my loneliness for when I was four years old my father gave me a little bear cub. I abandoned all my toys. I even stopped scrawling and daubing with pencil and paint all over my father's papers and books (although he scolded me for this, I had heard him telling friends, 'She's going to be an artist'). We became inseparable. I named him Mishka and taught him to drink milk out of a bottle. I would dress him up in my clothes and dance with him, and sometimes, when the dogs were locked up, Mishka and I would caper about the yard until I almost felt I was a bear cub too. This, the happiest time of my childhood came to an abrupt end.

To my misfortune a governess was hired, she took an instant dislike to my playmate. She began by teaching me to read and write and to behave nicely, not to eat noisily like Mishka, nor put my finger in my mouth. I was to dress like a well-brought up child of a good family: ribbons, lace, a clean pair of long pantaloons; but I liked to dress at my will. Father would laugh and say: 'I have no fear of starving to death, if I lose my job at the Ministry I'll take Mishka and Marie with me and we'll earn our living at the circus and the *balgan*. Look how funny and endearing they are!'

But the governess hated the bear and so did her daughter. The servants grew afraid and eventually she persuaded my father that it was all wrong for a little girl to be brought up with a bear. One day Mishka disappeared. I hunted high and low for him until I opened a cupboard and saw his skin stretched out on a board. Horror brought on hysterics, and I was ill for weeks, imagining in my delirium that my father would kill me as he had killed Mishka. I began to be afraid of him after he killed my friend the bear.

As soon as I recovered, the governess was dismissed and my father and I went to visit his parents in Warsaw. I made great friends with the old people. I slept with my grandmother in her big bed, and when she had attacks of asthma I rubbed her back and diverted her with stories about Mishka until she forgot her coughing and fell asleep with me in her arms. But this happy period too came to an end, and with it my real childhood.

9

My father was transferred to Tiflis, in the Caucasus and we made preparations to leave. In those days the journey was no rest. Mountain bandits descended on the road to attack travellers, rob them and sometimes to take possession of their wives and children. However the voyage to Tiflis passed off without incident, but the journey through those magnificent mountains filled me with emotion and amazement. Thanks to my travels with my father, my imagination was enriched and developed: I acquired a longing to see the whole world and all its strange people.

On arrival in Tiflis—in the incomparable landscape of the incomparable Georgians, with their brilliant costumes, their tales and legends, their songs and dances—we lodged with a bourgeois family who let my father two unfurnished rooms. I had to live with the family, with four girls older than me and one boy my age. Eventually the furniture arrived from home and my father installed himself comfortably in a study and bedroom. I found these rooms intriguing, they were filled with carpets and our red, gold and black painted furniture from the North of Russia. Nobody at Tiflis had ever seen furniture like it and people came to look at the strange beautiful chairs. On the walls hung a reindeer head with enormous pointed antlers and a huge boar's head with frightening teeth, other antlered heads and a fox. My father really did want me to grow up more like a boy than a girl.

The social life my father took up drove us apart; and, in the midst of this family, I learned the sorrows and terrors of a child deprived of the love of mother and father. I was taunted continually. 'Look at the savage! You can see at a glance she was brought up with dogs and bears. Look how she shows her teeth, as if she wants to bite somebody.'

Now the landlord's wife, whom I had to call 'my aunt' was a violent, screaming woman. She never beat me like she did her own children, but she threw scissors, plates, the iron or anything else that came handy at my head. I was always petrified but I learnt to play the same sort of dangerous game and I became hard and pitiless. I didn't deserve such terrible treatment but I was vulnerable. The woman was in love with my father (I learned afterwards) and the tenderness he showed me was torture to her!

I prayed God to help me. I dared not complain to my father, because I knew his violent temper. 'What if he kills them?' I thought.

Then I was sent to school, where I was happy. I discovered the great Russian writers—Pushkin, Lermontov, Koltsov, Gogol—and their works captured my imagination and enriched me immeasurably. I began to draw again, and my work always appeared at the school exhibitions. But the headmistress and the teachers were puzzled by my pictures of witches, devils and monsters, which tended to resemble themselves, and asked me why I drew as I did.

'Why, because it seems to me that everyone is like something.' I replied with a smile. 'Like a bird, or an animal, or a monster, and this is strange and funny. Why, I even see my father this way.'

Although the notices of my work in the newspapers made my father proud, he told me, 'Your old nurse did manage to stuff your head with nonsense after all. You concentrate on your geometry and algebra, my girl. That's what's most important'.

I could not see for the life of me why this should be so, and went on drawing and painting as my fancy dictated.

At the close of my school career, I received a shock that I cannot recall without emotion even now. Upon being given my school diploma, I saw that it was made out in the name of Vorobëva, not Stebelska; I discovered that I was not the legitimate daughter of my father.

Shortly afterwards, I was sent to Moscow to study art. Coming from Georgia, I viewed Moscow, with its ancient streets, painted houses and gleaming church domes, as the essence of Russia. I delighted in the great picture galleries, and I attended courses at the Stroganov school. But the severe Russian winter was too much for me; I spent weeks in bed with bronchitis.

Next my father sent me to Rome, which enchanted me. I wrote him long, ecstatic letters about the buildings and the monuments, about the museums and the paintings and the sculpture, about how different it all was from anything I had ever seen.

Then in 1911 I went to Capri, and there at the centre of a colony of writers and artists, many of them Russians, I met Gorki. Physically and morally, he stood head and shoulders above the rest. I adored him for his stories, his gaiety, his Russianness and his compassion. On his side, he seemed touched by my admiration, repaying it with warm sentiment and protection. One evening he talked to me of his childhood, and his harsh merciless grandfather who beat him as a little boy until he bled, so that he could neither walk nor sit and had to sleep on his tummy. And so I told him about my childhood and my first lessons in life and its cruelty.

It was Gorki who told me to sign my pictures Marevna, taking the name from a Russian fairy tale about a sea princess. 'No one else will ever have a name like that,' he said. 'Be proud of it and worthy of it.'

For a time, I thought of marrying Gorki's stepson Yura, who was deeply in love with me. However, after six lotus-eating months in Capri, I realized that I was making no progress with my work and decided to pursue my studies in Paris. I parted from Yura with regret, but without sacrificing his friendship, from which I was to draw sustenance for many years.

* * *

Chaïm Soutine was born in 1893 in the poor village of Smilovichi, near Minsk, a haphazard agglomeration of wooden houses, the best of them having painted shutters, white curtains and flower-pots in the window; the worst, tumbledown huts with sagging fences. There were numerous little gardens and orchards with apple, cherry and plum trees; a thunderstorm would leave mud ankle deep and puddles in which ducks and pigs splashed about and children floated in boats made of wooden crates. In summer, all the roads were covered with dust, in autumn, with slush and mud, and in winter, with snow, so that it seemed as though Smilovichi was all alone, isolated from the wide world. Fields and forests stretched out beyond the roads, luring the children out in summer to gather raspberries, mushrooms and nuts.

If I recall now what Soutine told me about his appalling childhood, I realize that my childhood could not have been identical. His father was a poor Jewish tailor who had difficulty earning a livelihood for his family of eleven children. Chaim, the youngest and weakest, was an ugly, sickly child, who was disliked by his father who often singled him out for beating. He found it hard to grow up among ten others. He went to bed hungry at night. Sometimes he would escape to the fields or the forest taking with him a sugar lump or a boiled potato. Only hunger drove him home, where once again he was beaten for thieving and running off. He was often ill from lack of food.

Years of malnutrition, sickness and ill-treatment left him nervous, sensitive, timid and reticent; his family considered him malicious, secretive, conceited, quick-tempered and often quite unmanageable. At school he fared no better than at home, for he was beaten there too.

But none the less, Soutine had his mother who tucked him up and kissed him goodnight, and gave him, without the others seeing, something to console him for being the least loved child.

'You know, Marevna,' Soutine said to me during our last meeting in Paris, I still feel upset—even today, when I think how much my mother went short for me. Feeding eleven children! More like twelve, for my father was like a child, always hungry and sometimes he would take a morsel off my plate for himself. It was awful for my mother to watch that. So she would go without, poor dear, and I'm convinced she died because she did without so much.'

Fortunately, Soutine had the world of a wondrous imagination to help him surmount the misery of his early years. Some aspects of his childhood made a profound impression on him, such as the celebration of the Sabbath, which Soutine recalled vividly and recounted to me in detail. The seven-branched candlestick would be lighted, and then the men of the family, all with beards and side-curls, wearing skullcaps and long kaftans, would form themselves into a circle while the women and children would seat

Soutine

themselves on benches against the walls. The men, arms around each other's shoulders, would begin intoning a slow chant, gently swaying from left to right, then from right to left, gradually speeding up the rhythm of the ritual song and dance until the chant became a sobbing moan and the figures in the circle could no longer be distinguished. Little Chaim would tremble with excitement and press himself against his mother's knee, he was moved to tears by the dizzying whirl of dancers and the sight of the enormous black shadows flitting over the walls and ceiling, lending a fantastic aspect to the scene.

If some children are marked for life by early miseries, others derive buoyancy from their childhoods. And so it is illuminating to contrast Soutine's childhood with that of Marc Chagall, whose father, a modest Vitebsk dealer in pickled herrings, was also Jewish and also had a large flock of children. There the resemblance in family life ends, for Chagall's household was a happy one, and its members lived, in the words of an old Russian saying, 'in a crowd without rancour'. Chagall's family were gay people, full of humour and whimsy. His uncle, a lively fiddler whom the painter depicted on canvas many times, belonged to the Hasidim sect, which postulated the harmonious union of God and man in the joy of living. Chagall's work is full of the love of life, while Soutine, brought up to believe in a God who chastised man, saw a harsher vision and painted with extremes of realism and fantasy.

In early childhood Soutine used coal and chalk, and later on coloured pencils, to draw portraits and figures of the people around him. This infuriated his father, not only because of the traditional Jewish hostility to representation of the human form but also because young Chaim was destined for the tailoring trade. Called 'slobberer' and 'parasite', the boy who yearned to pursue his creative visions was forced to spend his time sewing. Life was almost intolerable for him. In summer, it was possible to escape from the house to the forest, where he could forget the home atmosphere and give himself up entirely to seeing, hearing and dreaming; he gazed at the landscape and its colours, his imagination endowing trees and clouds with fantastic shapes. But in autumn

15

and winter, kept indoors by the cold, he was at the mercy of his family. In the one room where all gathered to keep warm, Chaim would sit bent over a table, sewing by the poor light of a smoking kerosene lamp, listening to talk of how hard it was to feed so many hungry mouths, of how Jews were beaten and robbed and mistreated by the police, or pogroms. Why? For what sins were Jews afflicted with such punishment? It was difficult to sort things out. He would steal occasional glances at the grim faces of the bearded men, at the weeping women, at the grimacing children; above all, at the grotesque shapes of the shadows flickering over the walls and ceiling, expanding and contracting, as in a kind of dance.

Soutine found sympathy in his mother and in the kind and wise village rabbi, who saw the potentialities in this boy with his passion for drawing. These two effected a release from the tailor's small, mean house, angry hand and cruel yardstick. When Soutine was sixteen, he was sent to Minsk with Michel Kikoine, another Jewish youth, two years older, to study art with the painter Kruger, who claimed that he could make fully-fledged artists of them in three months!

Unlike Kikoine, whose father, a bank employee, was able to help him, Soutine lived from hand to mouth in Minsk. But there were acquaintances of the rabbi to take an interest in his protegé; they offered Soutine meals and moral support, and gradually he collected a small circle of friends. No longer was he obliged to hide or withdraw into his private childhood world. No one nagged at him because he wished to create instead of sew. Minsk offered things to look at and things to learn. To be sure, the art school was not entirely satisfactory, since he had to do what his teachers required rather than what he wished to do; but then Soutine's heart and mind were idiosyncratic and would always be hard to fit into a mould.

After a year, the rabbi arranged to send Soutine and Kikoine to Vilna, which possessed a good library and offered a richer, more interesting artistic life. The two enrolled at the Fine Arts Academy, where they met and became fast friends with Pinchus Kremègne, another Jewish art student. Kremègne, like Soutine, was the youngest of a large brood, but had not suffered the same privations, for his father made a decent living by carving figures derived from Slavic folklore. Several years older than the other two, Kremègne assumed a protective attitude towards them, particularly towards Soutine.

The three years Soutine spent at the Academy did not go altogether smoothly. He did not like copying (not his strong point) or sketching and, in general, did not like to draw according to the precepts of the art schools of his time. He disliked his teachers' insistence on accurate execution in certain kinds of work and, being painfully sensitive and almost pathologically proud, resented their criticisms. Often there were noisy disputes between stubborn teachers and the no less stubborn pupil. But despite these obstacles, Soutine saw that his talent was developing; this aroused and fostered in him the self-respect inherent in, and essential to, every human being.

Another talent was developing as well. There are always people who enjoy standing drinks to half-starved students in order to laugh at their drunken antics, and, thanks to them, Soutine acquired the habit of drinking heavily.

And so, when his benefactors decided to round off his development by sending him to Paris, his digestion was already ruined and he had a diseased liver. In addition, he suffered from a nervous affliction of the left eye and from frequent attacks of some, as yet undiagnosed, malady.

* * *

In 1913, Chaim Soutine and Michel Kikoine arrived in Paris, Pinchus Kremègne having preceded them the year before. At first they lived in the Cité Falguière, but soon settled in La Ruche (the Beehive), a network of painters' and sculptors' studios in the passage Danzig. Here Soutine made the acquaintance of the sculptors Lipschitz, Archipenko, Zadkine, Oscar Mestranovic and Bulakovsky and of the Italian painter, Amedeo Modigliani. From the very first meeting, Modigliani enchanted Soutine as he had enchanted others. (Paul Guillaume wrote: 'Modi was all charm, all impulsiveness, all disdain, and his aristocratic soul remained among us in its many-coloured, ragged beauty.') The handsome Italian had come to Paris in 1906 at the age of twenty-two, after having worked in Naples, Florence, Venice and Rome. His thorough knowledge of Italian art made him an excellent guide at the Louvre, and he acquainted Soutine with the Italian primitives, with the quattrocento artists, with Giotto, Botticelli and Tintoretto—with all the masterpieces he himself most admired. He drew Soutine into a circle of brilliant young artists—the painters, Pablo Picasso and Diego Rivera; the poets, Jean Cocteau, Guillaume Apollinaire and Max Jacob—and the gifted composer Eric Satie. Modigliani's interest in the arts was by no means limited to painting. He loved music, read Bergson, Nietzsche and Kropotkin (*Memoirs of a Revolutionary*—Modi regarded himself as a socialist, though he took no active part in politics), and could recite Dante, Wilde, Verlaine and Lautréamont by heart. He possessed a great talent for sculpture, which was encouraged by Rivera, among others, and for a time came under the influence of Brancusi, the well-known Roumanian sculptor of modern forms. (I well remember the ruined house on the boulevard Montparnasse with a lot of good quality stone in the yard, where Modi worked for a time. We used to go and peer through the fence to watch Modi wield his hammer and chisel.)

Through Modigliani, Soutine met Zborowski, a Polish poet who had dragged out a wretched, dissipated, cocaine-saturated existence until an intelligent and sensible Polish woman took him in hand and married him. She urged him to promote the work of talented artists, and he did, becoming the patron of Soutine and Modigliani, among others.

* * *

I received my introduction to La Ruche—from the Russian sculptor, Bulakovsky, a member of the Russian Academy, where I began working soon after I arrived in Paris. 'Would you like to see the young geniuses in their beehive?' he asked me one day. 'It's a fine place, crowded of course, but the more the merrier. You'll meet some young men whose names will be famous in all the galleries of the world in ten years. They're living from hand to mouth now and glory and love are only dreams to them, but they are passionate and sincere in the service of art, and they are indefatigible workers.'

La Ruche was like a great cauldron, seething with vitality. Here Russians, Poles, Italians and Spaniards lived together, sharing their good and bad fortune. It was a wonderful place, and it fascinated me, but I did not want to live in it. The inhabitants were nearly all men, and I was a little frightened of them.

'Well, what is it you're afraid of, their youthful passions or their poverty?' asked Bulakovsky, somewhat mockingly.

I met the unsociable Soutine, the gay Kikoine, the charming little Kremègne: the trio of young Russian Jews who were seen everywhere together. Of the three, it was Soutine whose appearance made the deepest impression on me. His clothes, unlike the workmen's blue linen jackets and trousers favoured by the other artists, were beige, with red and blue neckerchiefs; I was told that he made them himself. Like the clothes of the other artists, they were always covered with paint marks. He was not good looking. He had a short neck, high shoulders, and he stooped. His face was broad and jowly, resembling a primitive wooden sculpture hewed out with an axe. His thatch of coarse, dark hair was cropped like a Russian peasant's, but a fringe came down to his eyebrows and concealed his large, protruding ears and low forehead. He had expressive dark eyes, sunken and tilted upward; the lids were red and swollen. His nose, narrow at the bridge, widened into a thick wedge. He smacked his thick lips when he talked, and flecks of white foam gathered at the corners of his wide mouth. He had a charming smile which involved his whole being, drawing one closer to him, but the smile exposed his unhealthy, dull, dead-looking teeth, greenish at the gums, and one wanted to say reproachfully, 'Oh, Soutine, you haven't cleaned your teeth'. His hands were his most striking feature—small, pink and soft as a child's. It seemed incredible that those hands could paint such vigorous canvases.

Kikoine I remember as always smiling or laughing, as exuberant as his fascinating work, which was greatly influenced by Van Gogh, it seems to me, but without as much of the torment as Soutine assimilated and without the extreme distortion that gives Soutine's work such distinction and strength. I found Pinchus Kremègne a most attractive person—serene, cheerful, sensitive and humane. He had already evolved an Expressionist style at the Vilna Academy, and for a number of years in Paris he had a deep influence on Soutine, who was apt to destroy anything that Kremègne criticized. Later, this influence lessened and the friendship between the two gradually came to an end, probably because of a basic temperamental incompatability. Kremègne and Kikoine reacted to the privations and trials of the early years in Paris differently from Soutine. They both married and had families, and their work acquired a deeper humanity, whereas Soutine remained fundamentally solitary and the sense of horror and protest in his painting intensified over the years.

It is unfortunate that two such talented artists as Kikoine and Kremègne should have been so largely eclipsed by the genius of their compatriot. Kikoine's gay palette and wonderfully expressive touch, which have given the world so many magnificent portraits and nudes, landscapes and still lifes, and the originality, the dazzling colours, the unique spirituality and humanity of Kremègne (that 'humble Colossus', as Waldemar George has called him) surely deserve wider recognition by the mass of the art-loving public, who, if it has heard of them at all, think of them as 'the poor man's Soutines'. Both painters are still active today and have exhibited all over the world.

* * *

Another Montparnasse painter I met was Moïse Kisling, a friend of Soutine and Modigliani. He was a Polish Jew from Cracow who had come to Paris very young. There was something Asiatic and exotic about his face, with its smooth, olive-tinted skin, its beautiful black eyes shaded by long lashes, and its firmly outlined red mouth; but it was the quivering nostrils of his small, well-shaped nose which revealed the turbulent and passionate character of the artist. He enjoyed great success with women, from artists' models to the society ladies whose portraits he painted, and his manner with all of them was cajoling and very free. He liked to pat beautiful women on the thighs and back with his little hands, as men pat a fine mare, a doe or a bitch; most of them, far from taking offence, were flattered.

Kisling was generally regarded as a charming human being, though he could sometimes be a little surly and even cynical. His nature encompassed the two extremes of the Jewish temperament, melancholy and an irresistible gaiety that sometimes became wild, to the extent of shattering vodka glasses at parties. In addition, he had the Polish spirit of combativeness, and was quick to provoke quarrels, fights and even duels. But after these 'fights to the death', the opponents would drink to their friendship—and drink mightily! Kisling's duel with Gottlieb, another Polish painter, was the talk of Montparnasse for a time. I, myself, witnessed a fight between Kisling and the Chilean artist, Ortiz de Zarette, a mountain of a man. At one point, Ortiz picked up a heavy marble table with one hand and prepared to hurl it at the head of his opponent, who had fallen to the floor. Certain murder was prevented only with difficulty, but a moment later everybody was drinking and joking together.

I greatly admired Kisling's self-discipline when it came to his work, which he took very seriously. Even when he stayed up carousing until five or six in the morning, he would rise at nine and begin working at his easel, not stopping until two or three in the afternoon. (No one had to lock him up in his studio as Zborowski often did with Modi, who, having swigged a litre of wine at home, was likely to saunter out to one of his favourite cafés and go on drinking there.) He spent some time at the Ecole des Beaux Arts, but belonged to that group of free spirits who detested the classical drawing of the old school, rebelled against copying plaster statues and busts, and left the Academy to pursue freedom in their work. Kisling's landscapes and still lifes with flowers and fish 'sing' with rich colour, though he did not slather his canvases with layers of paint as his friends and colleagues Soutine, Kremègne and Kikoine did. Kisling's work is most agreeable to the eye: it is romantic and melancholic, full of the nostalgia, sadness and reverie found in the work of so many Jewish artists.

Like Soutine and Modigliani, Kisling came under the patronage of Zborowski, and for a time the two Poles both lived in the same building on the rue Joseph-Bara, near the rue Notre-Dame-des-Champs off the boulevard Montparnasse. Kisling's studio served as a gathering place. Early in my Paris days I noticed that painters often liked to work together. Part of the reason was sharing the cost of a model, but there were psychological reasons as well. Modi, attracted by Kisling's charm and generous friendship, painted more willingly in the Pole's studio than in his own. After a working session, there would always be something to eat and drink. Soutine, spattered with paint and permeated with the smell of it, was a frequent visitor. Others came too, and an excited discussion of painting went on late into the afternoon. Sometimes I would drop in, entering an atmosphere thick with tobacco smoke, seeing faces animated by talk and wine. The latest works of Kisling, Soutine and Modi would be propped against the wall, and Zborowski would come up from the floor below with one end in view—to look at the pictures and calculate how much he could get for them, for he had begun to bet quite openly on painters, as if they were horses.

One day Kisling asked the poet why he didn't take me under his wing too. Zborowski said he had nothing against the idea, but he objected to the name 'Marevna' and suggested that I alter my father's name to 'Stebel'. 'It sounds all right, and no one will know that you're a woman. Dealers don't have confidence in women painters. A woman will paint for a while and then she'll stop—she'll fall in love, or marry, or have a child, or divorce.'

'But will Marevna automatically be protected from these tribulations if she becomes "Stebel"?' asked Soutine.

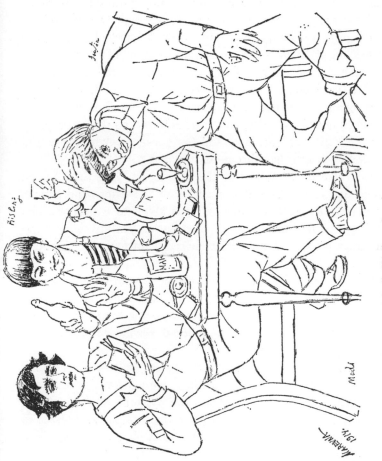

Modi, Kisling, Soutine

Everybody laughed, and nothing came of the idea. I did not want to corrupt my father's name, any more than I wanted to give up the name bestowed on me by Maxim Gorki.

I have a pleasant memory of an evening at Kisling's because it was so funny. I can see myself now, climbing the staircase to his studio, hearing laughter and the hubbub of voices. One would have said that all was jollity within, but when I knocked on the door silence fell, and I entered to the accompaniment of a Jewish dirge. Before me stood a kind of catafalque, illuminated by two candelabra, each holding seven candles. In the middle lay a huge book, open. Under the white sheet, a small, motionless body lay stretched out. To the left, on a huge sofa and on the carpet at its foot were gathered the host and his guests, looking grave and continuing to sing their threnody.

Who had died? Who was the little child lying there in the studio that had witnessed so many crazy gatherings and famous orgies? I felt uncomfortable, and was about to withdraw when Kisling, in a melancholy voice, asked me to put my signature in the great book. I complied, stealing a glance at the shrouded corpse.

'Poor little girl!' Kisling said in the same tone. 'The poor little thing is dead. We are assembled here to weep over her. She was beautiful, she was amusing, but her curiosity, her gluttony were too much for her. She loved, she suffered, she died. Peace be upon her soul.'

At this, laughter rang out. Kisling went up to the catafalque and threw back the sheet, disclosing to my astonished eyes the corpse of a big striped cat. It was the painter's own cat, whose unwholesome curiosity had led her to eat his paints. Unable to digest them, she had begun to swell and swell, and that morning had been found dead, her mouth smeared with paint.

When the First World War broke out, Kisling volunteered for the Foreign Legion, where he could give vent to his combative temperament, but he was wounded and invalided out. In 1915 he returned to his Paris studio, where an extraordinary surprise awaited him: a young American architect, Chapman Chandler, who had enlisted in the Legion at the same time as Kisling, had been killed, and had left the painter the considerable sum of 25,000 francs in his will. Kisling at once decided to go and work in Spain, but soon fell in with Marie Laurencin and the lame English poet, Arthur Craven, extravagant companions. The money was gone in a few weeks and Kisling came back to Paris.

In 1917 Kisling married Renée, who had an adolescent boy's beauty, with a face lit up by enormous doe-like eyes. They had two sons, Jean and Guy, born in 1922 and 1924. Their house at Sanaris, which the practical Renée turned into a pension, is still there, among its greenery and flowers—a reminder of that marvellous artistic period.

The Second World War found Kisling in Lisbon, where he underwent an operation, then in New York, where he had a studio overlooking Central Park, then in Hollywood, where he painted a portrait of Artur Rubenstein, then in Washington. In 1946 he returned to France, and in 1948, on the day after the opening of his exhibition at the Musée Grimaldi in Cagnes, he died of a stroke.

Kisling was particularly successful with his portraits, painting the children of the poor and the bodies of young women with the natural sincere tenderness and enthusiasm of a true artist. I have often heard people confronting these portraits exclaim, 'Oh, how beautiful!' And what more can an artist ask of his public than such spontaneous admiration, from the heart?

*　*　*

I also remember Mané-Katz very well; he was a tiny, dark man, who was often to be seen at the Rotonde or the Dome with Soutine, Kikoine and Kremègne. Extremely likeable, always smiling, and good-humoured, he slipped into our midst like a small genie. He was a Russian Jew, born in Kremenchuf in 1891, one of the eight children of a sacristan who wanted one of his sons to become a rabbi. Mané-Katz was sent to a seminary, where he became familiar with the world of ritual and ceremony, rich colours and materials,

25

the gleam of copper and the candles lighting up the shadowy temple—the background of his work and the source of his imagery. His studio in the rue Notre-Dame-des-Champs had a Biblical décor. There were seven-branched candlesticks, little copper lamps, a star of David, gold-embroidered chasubles, rustling priestly robes, liturgical tapestries. It seemed a magical world apart, in which the artist took refuge to paint, forgetting everything else.

Like Chagall, who in Paris and New York painted the scenes of his childhood and youth, Mané-Katz remained rooted in his past. Before the First World War he returned to Russia, where he was refused for military service because of his small stature. When the revolution provided openings for painters, decorative artists and theatre designers, he was appointed teacher at the Kharkov Fine Arts Academy, but the civil strife between Whites and Reds interfered with his life and work and he came back to Paris in 1921. Later, he disappeared from Montparnasse; we learned that he had gone to Israel, where he found a spiritual home. He became a popular hero and an official personage; a museum of his work was set up in Tel-Aviv. Although Mané-Katz travelled from one country to another, like the Wandering Jew, he always returned to Israel.

Mané-Katz went in for enormous canvases and monumental compositions. Active during the era of Cubism, he did not share the interest in spheres and cones that stirred so many other young artists. It was in Fauvism that he found his inspiration and the pure colours that radiated from his palette. He was influenced by Matisse and by the expressionists Münch, Kokoschka and Ensor. A visit to Japan at the end of his life and confrontation with the compositions and silhouettes of traditional Japanese art and with the non-figurative art of young Japanese artists showed him that a picture could be conceived in a few brilliant strokes. He did not abandon his devotion to beautiful technique and pure painting, but he gradually eliminated all detail which was likely to impair the plastic significance and tones of his work. Pierre Mazas wrote of him, 'Mané-Katz progressed with the knowledge of his art. He placed fewer and fewer "objects" on his canvases. His compositions became purer. Large patches of colour, four or five of them, sufficed to implant a country cottage out there—in the East, by a dirty river, under a bleeding sky.'

* * *

In those early days, Soutine and his friends would spend many evenings at the Russian Academy, which consisted of two rooms, one for sculptors and the other for painters, in the Impasse Avenue de Maine, behind the Gare Montparnasse. It was a meeting place for young emigrants from Kiev, Vitebsk, Minsk, Riga and Odessa, and there were also a few students from Finland and Estonia, and some from St Petersburg and Moscow passed through fleetingly. There were two woman painters besides myself from Tiflis—Olga Sakharova, a doctor's daughter, who was very talented, and Dagmar Mouat, half Georgian, half English, who drew very well. There was also an extremely gifted sculptress from Palestine, Chana Orloff.

At the Academy, morning sessions were devoted to oil painting and sculpture, and in the evenings everybody gathered in one room to sketch. Modigliani and other non-Russian artists used to attend these sketching sessions, which were always crowded. A nude model posed by the stove at one end of the room, and we drew in free style—what we wanted and how we wanted. Soutine always sat by the wall at the back, concealing the paper he was working on. I never succeeded in seeing a single one of his sketches, and sometimes wondered whether he ever drew anything.

On winter Saturdays, after the sketching, the samovar would be heated and we would all have tea. They made a pleasant picture, these young people, flushed with the warmth of the stove and the hot tea, conversing peaceably. Well, not entirely peaceably—there was always the resonant voice of Zadkine, known to us all as 'thundering Jupiter', to shatter the calm. The talented Zadkine, with his fringe of hair on the forehead and his marked

Semitic charm and wit, was bursting with energy and gaiety and could neither sit still nor be silent for long. Soutine, in contrast, was very quiet; a smiling countenance and everything about him showed that he was content in that atmosphere as he drank his tea out of a saucer, sucking it through a lump of sugar like a cab driver.

Another place where young artists gathered to sketch was the Colarossi Academy in the rue de la grande Chaumière. The crowd there, made up of all nationalities, was even thicker than at the Russian Academy, and all the rooms were generally packed. The clothed models—men, women and children—were usually Italian, and looked out of their element in the chilly fog of Paris, almost as though they had just disembarked from a voyage from Naples. In the room where we drew from the nude the air was stifling because of an overheated stove, and the model perspired heavily under the electric light, looking at times like a swimmer coming out of the sea. It was like an inferno, rank with the smells of perspiring bodies, scent and fresh paint, damp waterproofs and dirty feet, tobacco from cigarettes and pipes, but the industry with which we all worked had to be seen to be believed.

In winter, the Russian Academy sponsored charity balls for the benefit of needy Russian emigrants. The balls, instituted in 1911, were held in the great picturesque halls of the 'Moulin de la Galette', a *brasserie* called 'La Closerie des Lilas', and in the 'Salle Bullier'. There was a platform for performers—well-known actors and players from the music halls entertained before the dancing began—and two orchestras continuously played irresistible, jerky tunes or furious waltzes. The dance floor was surrounded by tables for those who wanted to dine or drink champagne, and all along the walls were chairs for the dancers to rest in. Sometimes there were boxes on the balconies, closed off with red velvet curtains and illuminated by dim, softly shaded lamps; these were reserved for lovers and for important people who wished to attend incognito. Everywhere were green shrubs, masses of scented flowers from the Côte d'Azur, cunningly woven garlands and many-coloured lanterns. Russian artists helped with

28

the decorations and also exhibited their canvases, which were auctioned off for the benefit of their needy compatriots. The all-important buffet, where I often helped out (when I was not moving through the crowd, selling glasses of vodka and hot honey), was situated at one end of the hall and consisted of several tables laden with an impressive selection of sandwiches and *zakuski* (Russian hors d'oeuvre) and a variety of drinks. Behind these tables were cordial, attractive ladies, ready to seduce 'customers' into eating the delicacies, the prices of which (as at all such charitable affairs) were exhorbitant and certainly beyond the reach of poor artists.

At eleven o'clock, the start of the evening, the atmosphere was always tense and uneasy as the ball committee awaited the arrival of the public. The people who came were a very mixed lot. The cream of the Russian colony came, and so did rich and eminent French society figures, industrialists and bureaucrats. Journalists and art critics were there in plenty, along with personalities like Lunacharsky, Chernoff and the young poet, Ilya Ehrenburg. When the hall was full, the performers did their turns, always having great success with a public that asked nothing better than to enjoy itself.

Then came the dancing. Where else could one find so festive a spirit as was to be found at our Russian balls? Nowhere. People thawed as they drank and inhibitions vanished. There were un-bridled *lezginkas*, performed to cries of 'Tash! tash! tash! tash!' and rapid clapping of hands, while dancers, as if hypnotized, whirled, bounded, capered round a single *danseuse* who hardly moved but provoked delirious paroxysms with her tantalizing gaze. Or perhaps the famous *kinzhal* dance, performed with the body stiff and the blade of a dagger gripped between the teeth. It needed only a cavalcade of unbroken horses to make me feel I was back in the Caucasus.

The painters often participated in the frenzied gaiety of the occasion. Some, like Kremègne and Soutine, never danced, but most of the young geniuses of the ghettos would become inspired by the strong *marc* that was circulating freely. They would rise from their seats to form a circle and, putting their arms around each other's necks or shoulders and lowering their heads, sway gently from left to right and from right to left and gradually pass into a rapid whirl, which one could not watch without emotion and without feeling a desire to enter into that living circle and become one with the dancers. Neither the religious melody nor the ritual dance was in the least appropriate to the general atmosphere of the balls, but I was always pleased to be given a glimpse into an unfamiliar, almost magical world.

Towards two in the morning the party reached its zenith. Everyone was enlivened by wine, looking red in the face and breathless. Dancers stumbled, and bursts of laughter became noisier and noisier. Slavs love singing, and choirs were improvised; I often participated. How beautiful the singing was! Nostalgia, dreams, suffering were all reflected in these Russian songs, and the people greatly appreciated them. The over-excited atmosphere, stimulated by alcohol, music and dancing, produced a general brotherliness. One could feel oneself becoming benevolent, happy and carefree.

At last, towards five or six in the morning, the excitement diminished, and the ballroom emptied rapidly. After so many hours in such a stifling atmosphere, the shock of going out into the fresh, icy air of those winter nights took my breath away. A damp, bluish mist seemed to swallow up the streets and houses, and nothing could be distinguished at a distance of ten paces. The lamp-posts with their gas-jets rose from the darkness, surrounded by a halo of pale orange light, dismal and uncertain. We walked in noisy groups, looking for an open café, and there, among pale, sleepy workmen, we waited for the Métro to open. In the streets, the ragpickers, men and women with baskets on their backs, looking like sinister humpbacks, rummaged about with iron hooks among the refuse bins, which were noisily overturned every now and then by stray dogs and cats, quarrelling over rotting remains of food.

Then, close on the heels of the workmen, we entered the Métro, to be greeted by the nauseating aroma of sweetish disinfectant. We felt awkward beside these men in their dungarees and shabby leather greatcoats or threadbare jackets; dispirited, gloomy, badly shaven, they regarded us with ironical indifference. Occasionally, one of them would say to me derisively, 'Well, my beauty, you'll have had some fun with the boys. They're lucky,' and I would laugh with embarrassment. I felt guilty in the presence of these men. They had risen early for work, while I would soon be in my soft, comfortable bed, forgetting the fatigues of the mad night, and a day's work would be lost.

These Russian balls did not always go by without disorderly episodes and brawls, and I must admit that often I was the cause. I had a hoydenish streak in my nature, and usually attended the balls dressed as a young *muzhik*, wearing boots, wide, baggy trousers, and the traditional shirt embroidered in red; on my head I wore a magnificent astrakhan *papakha*, a present from my father. I felt at ease in these clothes, and I enjoyed playing the clown. The thirsty dancers who bought my vodka and hot honey called me 'Stepka' and were always ready to have me join them in drinking to the health of our venerable Russia. Everyone liked me. Occasionally, someone liked me too well, as was the case with a gross, vulgar fellow, quite drunk, who wanted a kiss along with the glass he bought from me. He said he had paid enough to deserve a kiss (there was some justice in this claim), and he caught hold of me, crushed me against his great belly, and tried to force his mouth, greasy and full of saliva, against mine. I gave him a couple of rattling boxes on the ear. He pushed me away roughly, swearing, and I fell down, smashing the bottles and glasses on my tray, right under the feet of a dancing couple, who fell on top of me. The man was laid hold of by indignant bystanders and magisterially punished with a kick in the rear; in addition, he ended up with two black eyes and a torn dinner jacket. I, on the other hand, was fêted with champagne. A cut on my hand was dressed, and for the rest of the evening I displayed the bandage with great pride.

Once, having had rather too much of my own wares to drink, I was emboldened to offer free glasses to some of my colleagues who could not afford the millionaires' prices being charged for them. One of the ladies of the ball committee, who was in charge of the buffet, was standing behind a table laden with *zakuski*, watching me. I knew she disliked my youthfulness, my success with the public, everything about me, and now she seized the opportunity to discredit me in the eyes of the committee. 'Look here, Stepka,' she shouted. 'Your friends must pay just like everybody else. That's not very honest, what you're doing.' What was the use of wasting words? I took action. I shoved the table, overturning it and scattering *zakuski*, pastries and the rest. What a mess! Broken plates, and Russian salad mixed with vanilla ices. The lady screamed with rage. Some of the other committee ladies, astonished, evinced no sympathy for me, reproaching me bitterly and demanding that I be turned out at once. But I had my defenders. 'Turn out Marevna?' they said. 'Why, you can't treat her like that. She's always done her best for the committee. Something must have happened to hurt her feelings.' My anger passed, and I began giggling uncontrollably.

These Russian balls were children's games compared with the balls given by the artists from the Académie des Beaux Arts. I attended one in the company of two boys dressed as cavemen, myself a prehistoric woman with my hair loose on my shoulders and wearing two birds' nests as a *soutien-gorge*. When we got there, it was to find debauchery unlike anything I had ever seen before; I was so ashamed and revolted that I wept in spite of myself. My escorts, surprised and amused, suggested that we leave, but the thought that my reaction might be taken for hypocrisy induced me to stay.

In the middle of the night a fire broke out. The way people panicked and shoved was a harrowing sight, particularly the women, nearly all of them naked, who rushed out of doors uttering heartrending screams and trampling on each other like a herd of beasts. The fire was brought under control, but not before everybody was well dedaubed with acrid soot. At dawn, when the crowd began to disperse and we found ourselves in the street again, my friends and I looked more like demons than cave dwellers. I could not walk any more because of all the rounds and *farandoles* I had danced, so I was put in a wheelbarrow and wheeled around the yard of the Académie des Beaux Arts. One madman, who had not been sobered by the dawn, still had the strength to dance in the basin of a fountain. A beautiful girl stripped naked and hoisted herself up beside him to take a shower-bath under the icy water. It was the most lovely vision I have ever seen—in the gilded light of the rising sun, immortal Venus was being born of the waters, pink and russet, with her long hair loose.

'Hurrah!' someone cried. 'Long live beauty, art and love!' The cry was taken up and resoundingly echoed.

I was told the girl caught pneumonia as a result of this exploit and died in hospital a few days later.

* * *

Before the war, at the close of the *Belle Époque*, Bohemia gradually shifted from the rue Ravignan in Montmartre to the boulevard Montparnasse. Most of the young artists and students of Paris used to haunt the Rotonde, a small café at the intersection of the boulevards Raspail and Montparnasse. The Rotonde was more than a meeting place—we came together like one big family. The patron, old Leblanc, a former butcher, was a kind of father to the little colony that was always hard up and always in need of moral support, for life in Paris could be harsh, pitiless and lonely. In the Rotonde it was possible to sit all day over a single *café-crême* without being driven away; moreover, one could get *choucroute*, soup and ham sandwiches on credit. Leblanc would recoup his losses from his evening clientele of fat bourgeois and their wives, civil servants on the way home from the office, sweethearts and overdressed, overpainted *laides* waiting for clients. He also accepted sketches or canvases in lieu of payment, bought artists' pictures, and over the years assembled a fine collection, among which was a drawing by Foujito and canvases by Modigliani, Soutine, Kremègne, Kisling, Ortiz and others—and even one

33

At the Café Rotonde

of mine.

The Rotonde was the headquarters of some interesting members of the Russian emigré colony, of which Ilya Ehrenburg was the chief Montparnasse representative. Other Russian frequenters of the café were Markov, Aleksinsky, Savinkov and the poets Belmont and Voloshin. The gloomy Trotsky would look in to play chess with the equally gloomy Kandinsky, an architect who later became an abstract painter; these two dark, saturnine individuals, with their pointed beards and Mephistophilean profiles, alarmed us all because we took them for police spies, but then Ehrenburg set our minds at rest by identifying them for us. The muster roll of those who dropped in at the Rotonde reads like a list of anybody who was anybody or was to become anybody: Léger, Braque, Picasso, Soutine, Kremègne, Kikoine, Rivera, Gris, Picabia, Matisse, Modigliani, Max Jacob, Kisling, Apollinaire, Zadkine, Larionov and his wife Gontcharova, Vassilieva, Saugrade, Lhote, Favory, Metzinger, André Delhaye. One day Charlie Chaplin came in, wearing his bowler and swinging a black cape; the crowd surged toward him crying 'Charlot! Charlot' and literally carried him upstairs to the restaurant. This was truly the apotheosis of the café. Lenin came in once, but very quietly and without any ovations.

* * *

Ossip Zadkine was one of the people of whom I saw most during my early days in Paris. He came to my studio often, and when neither of us had any money, I would sell a load of empty bottles to buy some sausage and fried potatoes, or we ate bread and dripping or drank tea. Dazzled with each other and a little bit in love, we sometimes behaved like children, walking about the boulevards hand in hand, teasing each other, kissing and biting each other savagely. Sometimes we took the tram and escaped from Paris to the forest of Meudon, our favourite place in the country, and walked and walked. We would return to Paris with our feet covered with bruises, but happy. I have always thought that

35

Zadkine picked up his passion for walking—'le *footing*', he called it—in England, while he was at Oxford. I caught it from him, and I am proud of being able to walk several kilometres without getting tired.

Zadkine was a truly delightful companion, and the memory of his friendship is always with me. His love for his work was intense, and inspired me to work harder. He had great dignity and tremendous pride in his work. 'I want to revive Jewish art,' he would say.

Zadkine's temerity (one might even call it arrogance) was well-known; his friends and colleagues said he did not speak, he yelled or barked like a dog, and it was true. He was not always in control of his temper, as I found out one evening. We were out walking, and suddenly started arguing about art and about our work. He said something extremely rude to me and, furious, I smacked him soundly in the face. At once he paid me back in the same coin. I spat in his face and ran, aghast at what I had done. He came tearing after me. I ran until I was ready to collapse and then stopped, certain that he would disfigure me at the very least. His face was red and sweating and his eyes glittered fiercely. 'Think yourself lucky that you're Marevna,' he bellowed, 'for if you were anyone else. . . .' He waved a fist that looked as hard as iron, and we both burst out laughing. We never quarrelled again.

Late one night he arrived at my studio in the rue Méchain to tell me excitedly that at five o'clock in the morning there was to be an execution in the Santé. From time to time we could hear disquieting cries and screams from the prison, a hum of human voices rose from the boulevard.

'Do you hear the inquisitive wretches?' Zadkine said. 'I should like to throw a bomb amongst those who have gone to see this frightful spectacle. They say that the condemned are three horrible assassins, but the most horrible assassin of all must be in this crowd, which comes laughing to see an execution. Little crooks often pay the price for big ones, don't they?'

The two of us were feverishly upset and comforted ourselves

with kisses and caresses. Oh, life passes too quickly—we were living the happiest time of our lives. When we woke, the day was beginning to dawn.

'Shall we go and have a look?' asked Zadkine, lighting his pipe. 'It must be terrible.'

We rushed outside. A huge crowd was pressing against the big gate of the prison. The police restrained those in front. We stood on tiptoe to get a better view of what was happening. We could see the guillotine and the faces of the crowd, grey, with open eyes and mouths grimacing, reminding me of the faces in Goya's horror paintings of revolution and war. Zadkine's face was red and hard with rage. Suddenly there was silence, and three blows of the guillotine told us that justice had been carried out. The funeral cart drew away; the crowd dispersed slowly.

I also spent a great deal of time with Ilya Ehrenburg and his wife Katya, a small, boyish-looking woman with an interesting Byzantine face. At that time Ehrenburg's appearance was slovenly —a novelist's illustration of a nihilist. The pockets of his jackets and overcoats were invariably distended with newspapers and writing paper. His small, frail-looking hands, which might have been beautiful, were spoiled by nails discoloured with tobacco. His narrow, rather equine face was framed by long, greasy locks, and the collar of his jacket was usually covered with scurf. His full, sensual mouth, which twisted to one side when he spoke, was marred by several broken teeth, the result of having been arrested during his student days in Kiev—probably for political reasons— and beaten by the Russian police; he had never had the teeth mended, both because he was afraid of dentists and because he cared so little how his teeth looked that he seldom bothered to clean them. But one forgot all this before the captivating charm of his marvellous eyes, deep-set and luminous, with large irises and an expression that was humble (though I for one did not believe in the humility), wise and sometimes a little ironic.

Ehrenburg's parents were (I believe) German Jews. Born in Kiev in 1891, the only boy among four children, he was spoiled and naughty like most only sons. He used to boast to me of the

37

nasty tricks he played on his sisters. He would hide frogs or herrings in their clothes, tie their plaits to chairs when they were not looking and do anything else he could think of to make the poor girls cry. I always felt that if he had his childhood to live over again he would perpetrate the same torments.

It was not unusual for Ehrenburg to arrive at the Rotonde in the morning and remain throughout the day, writing poetry at his table. In the evening, he would read the day's output aloud. Sometimes the poetry aroused fierce controversy, in which the poet more than held his own, for his tongue was as agile as his mind and he had a mordant wit. More often, we were all greatly moved by his realistic poems, about love and the sufferings it engendered (he was very susceptible to women). Once he gave me a book of his poems *Le Canoun*, and asked me to illustrate the jacket cover. He himself possessed a remarkable talent for painting, and the ever-growing art collection of the Rotonde contained one of his water-colours. His illustrations of his poems and of his *Lives of the Saints* were done in bright colours in the Italian primitive style, and everyone who was given one was very proud of it. The water-colour of the life of St Mary of Egypt that he painted for me I kept for a long time; until someone filched it from me.

Ehrenburg had both friends and enemies in Paris, but even the latter had to admit his talent and his lively intelligence. Once, denounced for something or other by a treacherous member of the Russian colony, he was asked to go to the police station. On arrival, his everlasting pipe in his mouth, he found several of his books on the table beside the police officer, who behaved extremely civilly towards him. Gorki had a high opinion of Ehrenburg's talent. I have always admired his writing. Besides his poetry, I enjoyed *Europe Société Anonyme*, *Julio Jurenito*, *The Thirteen*, and, in particular, *Destin de l'Europe*, which is frightening to read because some of his predictions have come true.

Ehrenburg's friend and fellow poet, Max Voloshin, was also a good friend of mine. He was short and stout, with a big head that looked leonine because of his masses of dark, curly hair, his beard and moustache. His small grey eyes radiated intelligence, energy and humour. He dressed in velvet jackets and large, floppy bows instead of ties; at home he wore Grecian robes and sandals and a bandeau to keep his curls in place. He was extraordinarily clean and fastidious, neither drank nor smoked, and was very reserved in manner.

Voloshin's poetry was classical rather than realistic. A man of great culture and refinement, he was something of a philosopher too, being interested in India and Hinduism. His political views were most liberal, and he was as eager for others to enjoy liberty as to have it himself. It was a principle of his never to repay money he had borrowed from someone rich, but to make a present of that sum to a friend in need.

Like Ehrenburg, Voloshin had a great gift for painting and executed thousands of imaginary landscapes in water-colour. He never seemed to tire of painting mountains or piles of crags disappearing into fantastic clouds; plains running with rivers; forests with trees whose roots and branches had strange, almost human shapes. Always there was a storm, though a ray of sunlight filtered through the clouds to lend a kind of Dantesque mysteriousness to the scene. Once, marvelling at how he managed to turn out one dream landscape after another, I asked him how he did it. He looked at me quizzically, his little grey eyes sparkling, and confessed his secret. Every time he went to the lavatory, he took some paper with him, and by crumpling the sheets he made models of his landscapes. Crumpled tissue paper produced gentle, streamlined slopes, conjuring up marshes, brooks, stagnant water with low, swollen clouds and featherlike flecks of mist floating over them. Stiff paper meant mountains surging up with steep, smooth, sharp-edged cliffs and terrifying precipices. In this way, Voloshin assured me, he did not waste time during his sessions in the lavatory—in fact, he even spun them out.

A contrast to my flamboyant Russian friends was another Russian, Boris Savinkov, who was more conventional and did not like being laughed at. I met him through Voloshin, who presented him to me with the words:

'Marevna, I want to introduce a legendary hero to you. I know you have a zest for the extraordinary and for real supermen. This man is an exemplification of every beauty. You will be passionately fond of him.'

At first I did not like Savinkov at all. He gave me the impression of being solitary, withdrawn and proud. He was well-known in Russia and his fame had accompanied him to Paris, where he was introduced in drawing rooms as 'the man who assassinated the Grand Duke Michael'. Society women pursued him eagerly; I was surprised. Probably it was because of his reputation, not his looks. He was of average height, upright and slender, with a balding head and a long, narrow face. There were faint creases round his eyes, which sloped up towards his temples like those of our Kazan Tartars; when he talked, his eyes creased even more, leaving scant room between his almost lashless eyelids for his searching, ironical gaze to find its way out. Speech twisted his long, thin lips slightly, baring the yellowed teeth of a heavy smoker. He wore neither moustache nor beard, dressed very correctly and always wore a black bowler hat (at the Rotonde and elsewhere he was called 'the man in the bowler'). A large umbrella was always to be seen hanging from his left arm.

Savinkov's manner and way of speaking were impressive. Gradually my initial dislike faded and I became very fond of him. We met frequently, and on occasion he came to my studio to read to me from the volume of his collected work called *The Pale Horse*. His political commitment was intense, and he held very advanced views. In matters of aesthetics, his views were just the opposite— conservative, with a strong preference for classical art over modern. He was conservative as well about the antics of artists. Once, after I had taken him to visit Zadkine's studio, he complained:

'He's a buffoon, your Zadkine. Why does he act the clown?'

Zadkine's opinion of Savinkov was:

'An interesting personality, but why does he make himself out so important? Everything's finished for him in Russia.'

* * *

One day, at the Rotonde, M. Minkevich, a Polish copyist, was introduced to me, and asked me whether I could make him a copy of Courbet's landscape, 'La Forêt aux Biches', in the Louvre. I had never done a copy before, but I believe in the Russian proverb 'courage will storm a city'. I was then twenty-one years old and wanted to get on. I accepted. In preparation, I went to the Louvre to study Courbet's pictures, bought a book about his methods of work, consulted an English painter who had copied several masters, and considered myself ready.

To be sure, it was not entirely as simple as that. There were obstacles. The man who had ordered the copy from Minkevich, a Polish count, who wanted several copies of masters for his new *château* near Warsaw, had doubts of my ability because of my youth. Minkevich, extolling my talent with warmth and enthusiasm, overrode them. And then I had to endure the advances of Minkevich. Oh, only kissing my hand, as Poles like doing, but the pressure of his damp fingers was repugnant to me. So was everything else about him: small, burning black eyes; enormous, quivering nostrils; cruel, almost lipless mouth; big ears. My Montparnasse companions warned me against him, telling me that he had a reputation for paying his assistant copyists badly, when he paid them at all, that he was a heavy gambler and cheated at cards, that when in a rage he was capable of violence, which had earned him punishment more than once—and much, much more.

But youth is ambitious. Believing firmly in my own capabilities, I reminded myself of the Russian proverb and prepared a large canvas for my copy. My preliminary studies were completely successful, and my canvas was put in the Courbet room at the Louvre. 'Le Forêt aux Biches' was hung very high on the wall, and I was furnished with a stepladder. I was a striking sight, perched up in the air in my bicycling culottes and white socks. There were always people around me. The old Louvre copyists would come to assess my work, to criticize and to praise (I heard them say that I had great facility). Minkevich would come to see how the work was progressing and, overhearing the praise, go to fetch me tasty sandwiches or fruit. Other onlookers were the curious, many of them from the provinces, and their comments were a source of much amusement for me.

'She has more paint on her face than on her palette.' (And yet I never used make-up.)

'Look, she's wearing flowers in her hat. Are they real? Ask her if they're real.'

'Mademoiselle, are those flowers in your hat real?'

'Why, of course,' I would reply with haughty dignity.

Several times I observed Soutine standing nearby, alone or with friends. One day I asked him what he thought of my copy.

He told me frankly that he found my temerity and arrogance in copying Courbet, a painter he adored, astonishing and a little annoying. 'I am surprised that one so young should have undertaken to copy this masterpiece so boldly and rapidly. But so far everything is all right—the pattern of the trees, the animals, the stream and the stones. If I were copying it, though, I would certainly paint it in my own way, and I would breathe more life into the forest.'

I could see what he meant. My copy of the landscape lacked life, movement and artistic fervour, and everything in the picture seemed frozen in place, as in a photograph. I can imagine the forest as it might have looked if Soutine had done the copy: the trees would be bent over, their branches creaking in the wind; four fantastic does would be leaping beside the stream; the stones in the stream would be depicted as the grimacing heads of monsters.

My days were so well filled that my conscience could reproach me with nothing. I worked at my copying all morning and lunched peacefully by myself in a small workman's restaurant for one franc twenty-five or one franc fifty. After that I would work till four o'clock or as long as the light lasted, and then some friend or other would come to take me for a walk, to see an exhibition or drink a cup of coffee. In the evenings I went to the Academy to sketch.

I could very well have been contented with such a steady life, with being sensitive, idealistic and natural, had it not been for my ardent nature, which made it more and more difficult for me to

42

maintain my reserve forever. My nature, added to the fact that I lived surrounded by men—and artists at that. I had no desire for marriage or children; the idea of being shackled to a family frightened me. I saw in it the loss of my cherished freedom and the cramping of my work, and work for me counted more than anything. None the less, I could no longer stop myself from learning what love was, as everybody finds out in the end. I was old enough, I had no desire to be an old maid, and everything in me, soul and body, was longing for a man who could give me confidence and make a woman of me—a happy woman, but no man's slave. And that was precisely the difficulty. I should have to have faith in such a man, and in none of those who surrounded me—and God knows there were plenty of them—did I see 'the man in my life'. But as a result of knowing all these men I grew up and matured, my critical faculty developed and a personal point of view took shape.

* * *

In January of 1914, coming home late in the evening, I saw a telegram under the door. Something prompted me to leave it alone. Why, I asked myself, why does one always rush at the bit of blue paper delivered by the concierge or slipped under the door. I was tired after my day of copying at the Louvre. I had spent the evening with friends, and had suffered a headache the whole time. My friends had left me, and I had come home alone by the last Métro. Now my head ached fiercely; I felt strangely heavy and glum. I went to bed without opening the telegram.

The next morning I rushed at the bit of blue paper. It was from an uncle and informed me of my father's death.

My initial reaction was incredulity. My father could not treat me like that—die so suddenly and leave me all alone in life's jungle without a word, without a warning. I had to read the cold phrases again and again before I took them in. It was true. It was not a practical joke that someone was playing on me. My father was dead. Far away, so hopeless, so weary that he had been unable to hold fast to life and wait until we could meet again. What had happened? What had been the cause, the occasion of his death? Gradually, with comprehension, the tears came. Shudders overran my body. I lay in the early morning darkness half naked, prostrated by the acuteness of my grief.

Another telegram came, advising me to stay in Paris. What was I to do? Perhaps if I had had any money I should have set off at once. If I had tried to borrow the money for the journey, doubtless I could have found it. By my sorrow deprived me of any desire to act. Now that Father was no more, what use was anything? What could I do at Tiflis, alone and poor, faced with people who were strangers to me by now?

A letter followed the telegrams. A strange, hurtful letter, declaring that Father had committed suicide because of me and that I was a heartless and unscrupulous girl. 'I found your letters among your father's papers,' my uncle wrote. 'They reveal your lack of gratitude and affection. You did not love your father, who did so much for you, who lived for you alone. . . .'

I was bewildered by this. Those hard words were untrue. I had loved my father. I was convinced that some unknown cause had impelled him to perform such an act. A physical decline? A moral burden too heavy to bear? Clouds of menace on the political horizon? I was not able to find out; I still do not know. Perhaps everything combined to crush my father's spirit and in a moment of deep depression he succumbed. I was far away, and he had nothing to cling to. I could not help feeling guilty.

For several days I shed so many tears that I could see nothing; I lost my voice from wailing and sobbing. I stayed in bed without food, without purpose, without the courage to act, thinking that since my father was dead, I should die too. I neglected everything. I forgot everything. I was indifferent to everything.

One morning on the stroke of eight I was roused from a torpid sleep by loud crashes on the door. Then it shook violently, and a voice—Minkevich's voice—growled at me to open up immediately. I whispered to him in my ruined voice to have patience for a minute while I dressed. Possibly he did not hear. He began to

44

shout abuse through the door, accusing me of stealing his money (he had given me an advance on the copying), of being a lazy, drunken slut. Without a voice I was helpless before his tirade.

He broke the lock with a blow of his shoulder and stormed in, globules of saliva at the corners of his mouth as he continued to fulminate, his black coals of eyes searching the room for the lover he accused me of harbouring. I could not defend myself. Even with a voice, I could not have shouted loudly enough to summon the concierge; without one, I could not deny anything or explain. I seized an umbrella standing against the wall and whacked him over the head.

Minkevich was not slow to retaliate. Wrenching the umbrella out of my hand, he beat me with it. He beat me and beat me until the umbrella broke and I was on the floor. Then he threw the pieces away and dashed out.

In despair, wanting comfort and sympathy, I dressed somehow and went out to the Rotonde. I was so disfigured by tears and bruises that my friends could hardly recognize me. I told them about my father and about the beating. I got the comfort I was seeking, much of it from Katya Ehrenburg. I got more than comfort—a promise that I would see the Pole chastised for what he had done to me.

The act of vengeance took place late one evening at the Rotonde, where Minkevich was in the habit of dropping in for a game of chess. The café was crowded, and the faces I saw from the corner where I sat with Ehrenburg and Katya were the faces of well-wishers and sympathisers. When Minkevich walked in, several faces turned in my direction to give me smiles and winks of complicity.

It was an English painter friend who began it. He went up to the Pole's table and asked him for five minutes' conversation—'in the street'.

Minkevich, who sensed the hostility in the air, turned pale and refused.

'Are you afraid to come outside?' was the rejoinder.

'Afraid? Me? Why should I be? I've done nothing wrong. My

conscience is clear.'

'We shall see,' said the Englishman tersely, and propelled Minkevich gently but firmly towards the door.

Half the customers were on their feet, watching.

Minkevich was looking a bit greenish by now. 'What do you want with me?' Then, as somebody gave him an explanation: 'Marevna? Yes, I had a quarrel with Marevna. But nothing serious happened, I give you my word. No, I didn't hit her. No, of course I didn't know her father was dead. But I didn't hit her. I never hit her.'

In the face of these lying denials, the Englishman lost his self-control and gave Minkevich a punch on the chin, another in the eye. Then all at once there was a rush and everybody seemed to leap at the Pole, slapping, punching, even kicking.

Suddenly there was a pistol shot, followed by police whistles and shouts from the crowd that had gathered at the door. The brawl was over. Minkevich lay on the ground, a fearful sight— covered with blood, eyes closed, mouth swollen, nose a pulp.

'There, you scum, see what beating a woman has cost you. Take a good look at her. Open your eyes, you swine, and look! . . . Yes, officer, he's a swine. He beat a woman within an inch of her life and he wanted to shoot at us. Fortunately the gun went off in the air . . .'

One of the painters was doing the talking. It must have been convincing, for the policemen shoved the deflated Pole into a taxi and took him away. The mob of spectators dispersed, and the habitués of the Rotonde returned inside, laughing and triumphant.

Père Leblanc, who had not been a party to the plot, was very much upset by the unfairness of the fight—fifteen against one! He reproached me with maliciousness for allowing such a slaughter to be perpetrated on my behalf. But when Ehrenburg gave him an account of what had happened, he declared that if Minkevich ever set foot in the Rotonde again he would be thrown out on his ear.

Right after this I fell seriously ill. No physical cause was ascertainable; it was my soul that was sick. I seemed to have lost the taste for living. When I was at my lowest ebb physically I received a letter recounting in detail how my father had died. Just before the end his health had declined and he had shown clear symptoms of neurasthenia. He had spent much time shut up in his bedroom, and one day there had been a loud noise behind the closed door, to which no one had paid any attention. Only when he failed to respond to a summons to dinner was the door opened, to a strong smell of gunpowder. Someone had gone in. (What someone? Who had been the first to see him? The letter did not say.) Bronislav Vikientievich Stebelsky lay on his bed under two icons of Christ. He no longer had a recognizable face or head. All that was left of him was his tobacco-stained moustache. With his favourite rifle, he had fired a bullet into his mouth.

Poor Father. Today I can think of him calmly and tenderly, but I still regret that I was not able to see him before the end. Perhaps if we had met again he would not have yielded to despair, but died peacefully of old age, like his father before him.

Before he died, Father had sent me my monthly allowance, along with a parcel of Caucasian cheese, *halva*, dried fruit, picture postcards of the Caucasus, a fine carpet, and his magnificent white silk tussore cap, which I had long coveted (I wept upon seeing it). The money was soon gone. Any valuables my father left were seized upon by other members of the family, who were on the scene—as I was not. His life insurance, after being apportioned among his surviving relatives, was to bring me only a few dozen francs a month for about a year. But I was saved from destitution by my friends, who organized a charity ball for my benefit two months after my father's death.

I remember the ball very clearly. It was held in a big café in the avenue du Maine. I was not supposed to attend (indeed, I was not even supposed to know about it), for my health was poor and I had a fearful cough. But the solitude of my room, combined with the persistent dejection I had been feeling since my father's death, was too much for me. I decided to go to the ball, but not as Marevna. I smeared my face with ochre mixed with black, also my neck, chest and arms. I flattened my breasts with a towel and put on a nightshirt. A sheet folded in half and wrapped around my waist, slashed at the bottom and gathered round my ankles made a baggy pair of trousers, and a flaming red scarf—with a Caucasian dagger tucked inside for good measure—held them up. I piled my fair curls on top of my head, inverted my salad basket over them, and wound a strip of linen around it—a most striking turban. Two curtain rings served as earrings. When I had put black round my eyes and rouged my lips, I did not recognize the pirate lad who looked back at me out of the mirror. Nothing—absolutely nothing—was left of the Marevna of the Russian fairy tale. I was sure no one would know me.

It was past midnight when I was ready. I wrapped myself in a long, full red and green kimono (a present from Madame Gorki) and set off, walking with a jaunty masculine gait, both because I wished to enter into my part and because the avenue du Maine was in a district of bad repute.

No one at the ball recognized me. Everyone was intrigued. Though fancy dress was the order of the evening, masks were off by the time I arrived and most of the disguises had been penetrated. I was a complete mystery.

'Hullo, a blackamoor! . . . What's your name? Ali Baba? . . . Astonishing get-up. Who on earth can that chap be?'

I enjoyed myself thoroughly. I made up to the women, pretending to be much smitten with them. Without uttering a word (there was danger in speech, of course), I kissed their hands, stroked their shoulders, made signs to show how much I admired their hair. With the men, I swaggered, jostled, simulated rage even to the extent of drawing my dagger—all this without a smile, though at times it was not easy. I had a few bad moments when Zadkine and two ladies surrounded me.

'We must undress him and take his turban off,' one of the ladies said with a laugh.

I put my hand on the dagger and adopted a threatening air. They wanted to make sure of my sex by touching my breasts, but this I would not permit. As evidence of masculinity I displayed my hands, which were strong and slender and more like a boy's than a woman's. I also let them feel the banana I had been fore-sighted enough to place inside my trousers. Zadkine looked at me with obvious puzzlement and said there was something about me that gave him the impression he had seen me before somewhere.

I tried to stay away from people I knew too well, and succeeded. No one suspected my identity. None the less, after the initial pleasure of fooling everybody faded, I felt exhausted and de-pressed and retreated into a corner. I had no money and could not stand myself a drink, and I was too proud to accept the drinks that were offered to me. Later, when people began to disperse, I joined the group who were going to the Rotonde for the inevitable *café-crème* and hot *croissants*.

Seated at a table with the Ehrenburgs, Zadkine and a few other close friends, I enquired—in a hoarse croak—where Marevna was, and received the explanation that she was ill at home and ignorant of the ball being given in her behalf.

'Oh, no, she isn't,' I said, pulling off my turban. 'You see she's among you all the same.'

Everyone was much surprised, and the secret of the banana aroused merry laughter.

'You are hiding your real gifts, Marevna,' said Ehrenburg. 'Considering what life really is, you remind me of a fallen angel, or a raging madman, or a badly tamed tigress. Tonight you showed yourself to us as a well-camouflaged devil.'

There was more laughter, followed by a toast to my health. Then we all warmed ourselves with coffee.

The sun was just rising when I set off on the walk home. The street-sweepers were beginning their cleaning of the boulevards. Groups of workmen were hurrying to catch the first Métro. Other workmen were cycling out to the suburbs. My attire provoked laughter and remarks were passed, some funny, some indecent. The coolness of the morning, fragrant with fresh and pleasant smells, made me shiver. I also shivered because of my approaching departure. I was going to Italy to get my strength back. I had mixed feelings about leaving Paris—Paris, which had sometimes treated me cruelly but more often amassed a store of memories

49

Parade, rue de la Gaîté, Paris

Modi, Soutine, Rivera, Marevna, Voloshin, Ehrenburg, Picasso, Max Jacob

that I would cherish for the rest of my life.

It was a glorious era to live through. Much of the excitement stemmed from being young, from being part of a group that shared similar aims and ideals. And what a group it was! Our mere appearance on the street caused no end of commotion, and small wonder. Generally in the lead was the dark, bearded giant, Diego Rivera, striding along with tremendous dignity and brandishing his Mexican walking-stick decorated with Aztec figures. I came next in a wide-brimmed pink Italian hat, my father's cape, bicycling culottes held up with a wide Neapolitan belt (another gift from Gorki's wife), short white socks and black slippers (a marvellous outfit, as I could see in all the shop windows we passed). Then came Modigliani, with his wonderful curly Renaissance head, his shirt open to the waist, a book in his hand, declaiming passages from Dante's *Inferno*. Soutine followed, his long fringe reaching down to his eyes, a *caporal* cigarette between his lips, red-faced and beaming after a good dinner with plenty of wine (when he was out of sorts he kept to himself). Also in the procession, the horse-faced Ehrenburg and the leonine Voloshin, and Picasso and Max Jacob brought up the rear—the one in his enormous checked 'cubist overcoat' with an outsize jockey's cap on his head, the other in a waisted coat, black top hat, white gloves and spats. The amusement of the street urchins knew no bounds, and they would run up ahead of us to get a better view, shouting, 'Hey, look, it's the Cirque Medrano! Look, there's the giant with his club! Look at the animals and the clowns! And just look at the Musketeer's daughter with her pants and her wig!' (This last annoyed me—it was my own hair!)

Need I say that in those days we were all leading an existence far removed from real life? The whole world seemed to be intoxicated with art. Typical of the times was the enthusiasm aroused by the Diaghilev ballet: by the dancing; by the costumes and décor designed by such great artists as Larionov, Gontcharova, Benois and Bakst; by the music of contemporary Russian composers; and, above all, by the genius of the impresario in fusing the elements into a harmonious whole. We witnessed the shocking première of *Le Sacre du Printemps*, when large sections of the audience booed, whistled and shouted for their money back. Then there was *Parade*, a ballet designed by Picasso in which the dancers were dressed in cubist constructions and the music was provided by the tapping of heels. The first performance virtually caused a riot. Fights broke out in the auditorium, hard punches were exchanged, and all of us who were Picasso's friends waded in, trying to eject the trouble-makers. The police had to intervene to restore order. It is hard to imagine now that a theatrical performance could arouse such violent passions.

And so it went on. We were young, deeply committed to art, confident in our talents and our powers, united in our desire to spurn everything we saw as prosaic and bourgeois. To be sure, we all had our share of difficulties and disasters. A number of artists gave way before them, like those who turned to drugs for oblivion or illusory relief, and perished through their inability to break themselves of the habit. But most of us still had the youthful energy to surmount our tribulations—to survive, to live, to work and, of course, to love!

II
Diego and Marevna

Diego and Marevna

In 1914, when war came, life in Paris suddenly became very hard, especially for foreigners, students and artists. In the early days of the war, officials of the Ministère des Beaux-Arts came round to visit artists, to find out how they were faring, what they needed, and to check on the justification of claims for assistance. Artists were asked how they had lived before the war, whether they had received subsidies, from whom, how much and for what. Even foreign artists benefited from this aid.

As the war dragged on the French government was gradually obliged to withdraw all the privileges that had been granted to foreign artists, in order to extend them instead to French families, which numbered more and more widows and orphans. But the artists somehow managed to avoid starving to death, came to each other's aid, and went on working in expectation of a better life. Many French artists—among them Braque, Léger, Favory, Metzinger, Lhote and Saugrade—joined the forces, some out of patriotism, others for sheer love of combat and adventure. Of the Russian and Polish artists, Kisling, Zadkine and others joined the Foreign Legion; Ehrenburg and Savinkov became war correspondents and wrote some outstanding reportage. The French and foreign artists who were not sent to the front were exempted for various reasons: one had flat feet; another had a finger or two missing; Modigliani was predisposed to tuberculosis; Soutine had a stomach ulcer, was subject to fits, and had a defective left eye.

55

It was rumoured that the artists, especially the Poles, fought well in the front line. Those who were invalided out and came back to Paris continued to fight their battles at the Rotonde. Braque was wounded and discharged with a decoration. Fernand Léger used to send his wife Jeanne marvellous drawings of the battlefields: intricate compositions in ink of the muzzles of cannons, shells, pipes and other paraphernalia of war; telegraph poles lying diagonally across distorted felled trees which resembled water pipes. The painters and art lovers were all fascinated by this war seen in tubular form. When Léger too, was wounded, he returned to Paris; after his recovery, he continued to paint in the same style.

Others began to come back from the front, wounded or, more often, gassed, as were Favory and Metzinger. Apollinaire received a head wound, from which he died two years later. As he lay in hospital, white as a sheet, with his head bandaged, he smilingly showed us the bullet hole in his cap and said he would stay alive out of spite, to write a poem called *Gloire aux Allies*. Just as Léger depicted the war in new forms, so Apollinaire described it in a new form of poetry. Our friend the writer, Blaise Cendrars, who lost his left arm nearly to the shoulder, remained as gay and witty as ever. Picasso once said of him, 'He's lucky, that Blaise Cendras. He's lost one arm and found three!'

On returning to Paris from Italy at the end of 1914, I hardly recognized the quiet, empty town. These were hard times for me. I no longer had financial support from my father. Moreover, the Louvre was closed and I could not finish the copy of Courbet (ultimately, it vanished—no one ever found out what became of it). I went straight to the Rotonde, and there—O miracle!— Père Leblanc lent me money to rent a studio in the rue Asseline.

In winter, through the cold, short and often hungry days, we hung about in the Rotonde from morning to night. What else could we do? Where else could we go? Few of us were in the position of Ehrenburg, who lived in a hotel and had heat and hot water during certain hours; but then he earned the right to live like a bourgeois for part of the day by hauling crates and sacks at the station at night. Most of us were chronically short of coal and gas and had long since fed to the stove all that could be burnt; the water in our studios was frozen. After a night spent shivering under thin blankets, we would rise late and rush to the café, to be greeted by a kind smile and a *'comment ça va, mon petit?'* from Leblanc. Everyone was here. Bohemians. *Filles de café.* Even soldiers on leave from the front (alas, these heroes brought with them lice and other disgusting insects—getting rid of these pests was a most unpleasant procedure). We would crowd at the door of the toilet to wash. Then we would warm ourselves with hot coffee and croissants, read the news from the front (perhaps the war was over!), talk about the war, about Russia, about exhibitions and about the art that was not extinguished but whose spirit (and a few crazy buyers) helped us to survive. If we had the money, we would go to the Colarossi Academy to sketch; here reigned a pleasant warmth and an almost religious silence that struck us forcefully after the Rotonde, where passions seethed and churned. We worked away, trying to forget the war, the Spanish Influenza, the bombardment that Paris was undergoing day and night.

But the war was always with us, and we all suffered from it. Without my friends, I do not know what I should have done at this time. One day Soutine and Kremègne asked me how I was faring, whether I was selling my pictures, and whether I had a steady buyer for them. I had to confess that I was in a bad way. Kind Kremègne then insisted on giving me a reliable address, on condition that I did not disclose it to anyone else. Early in the month, I was to go to the main Préfecture of Police, where there were two art-loving commissioners who bought pictures from artists nearly every month. I went, and on the walls of the office I was shown into I saw still lifes by Soutine, Kikoine, Kremègne, Modi, Valadon and her son Utrillo (purchased, I discovered, for about fifty francs apiece). My work made a favourable impression on the commissioner, whose name was Léon Zamaron, and from then on I would always go to his office once a month with a picture. Sometimes, when Zamaron had lost heavily at poker, to which he was passionately addicted, I was sent to some 'guilty' client of his with a note from him; the client would make haste to buy my picture.

Kremègne and Soutine indeed helped me to keep the wolf from the door. Others helped as well. Gustave Kahn, of the newspaper *Le Quotidien*, took a great interest in my work and bought many pictures from me. He often told me: 'You have the stuff in you to make a great painter, Marevna.'

One evening Voloshin introduced me into the salon of M. and Mme S., who were enthusiastic patrons of the arts. Before we entered Voloshin said, 'Don't be too naughty. I shall do all I can to see that Mme S.—and her mother too—buy pictures from you. Only you must smile and show your teeth merrily. Don't scowl.'

Beautiful, tall, and majestic, Mme S. sat enthroned among the guests, the majority of them men, guiding the conversation, which revolved around artistic and political questions. I thought her too talkative. She wanted to put herself forward, at all costs, as a connoisseur of art—especially modern art. At one point Savinkov whispered to me, 'What a pity that such a pretty woman should open her mouth!'

At first I felt rather out of my element in her sumptuous rooms with their magnificent carpets and valuable furnishings. It was odd to see Ehrenburg, with his dirty shoes and long hair, knock out his pipe wherever he chose. He observed me looking at him and called to me loudly, 'Now, Marevna tsarevna, what are you looking at me like that for? Don't I look a perfect picture, seated in this red silk armchair?' I laughed.

Gradually, I lost my shyness and came to love those evenings round the great table laden with food and drinks, where I listened to these soul-stirring personalities assert themselves. Rivera, chewing slowly, delivered long, fascinating discourses on painting and politics. Voloshin supplied vigorous rejoinders. The reserved Savinkov listened to the others talk with an ironical expression. But he enjoyed himself too, and I knew it was a pose when he said that he was fed to the teeth 'in the ridiculous *salon* of the buxom, lion-hunting Mme S., who was determined to play the Maecenas to artists'.

* * *

In those difficult days artists and emigrants were helped out by two Russian canteens. The first of these, in the boulevard Montparnasse, was opened by Delevsky, a former Russian naval officer, who had been wounded in the leg during the first revolution in St Petersburg, after which he emigrated to France. In Paris, he and Sazonov played an active part in emigrant affairs, setting up the Turgenev Library, among other things.

At Delevsky's canteen the food was simple, but copious and tasty. Delevsky used to say that to put butter in the *kasha*, he first had to buy butter, and that he therefore had to charge for meals, but the prices were negligible: sixty centimes for a bowl (or two) of soup; ten centimes for a glass of tea with sugar; meat, *kasha* and bread were free. Hungry artists quickly followed the emigrants to the canteen, characteristically seeking credit, but Delevsky was firm. 'My friends,' he would say, 'I'd be delighted to feed you all free of charge. You'd all be welcome. But in two or three weeks there'd be no more money and I'd have to close the canteen. And then where would we all be?' But he did not rule out credit altogether, allowing it to a chosen few. Soutine was one. 'He's talented, the devil take him,' Delevsky would say, chewing at his fair, curly beard. Nor was Modi turned away, if he came sober. Delevsky served no wine in the canteen, a source of some annoyance to Modi.

I remember a young Jew who came to the canteen several days running. It was said that he was walking to Palestine. He appeared in a tattered old coat, a threadbare jacket without buttons, no shirt and trousers frayed at the ends and belted with rope. His red-gold hair fell in long curls to his shoulders. He kept his small hands in his sleeves, and his bare feet, blue with cold, stepped lightly on the dirty, frozen asphalt. Delevsky told the cook to serve up a large bowl of cabbage soup with two or three pieces of meat in it, a plateful of bread and a glass of tea with lemon. Without a word, the Jew began eating, smacking his lips loudly: first the bread; then the soup; then the meat, using a knife and his fingers to push the pieces into his mouth; finally the tea. Afterwards he cleaned his teeth with a fork without looking at anyone, heaved a sigh and belched loudly. With a shy look at Delevsky (the eyes of both men were shining), the Jew left the canteen without paying.

The first time this happened we all sat dumbfounded. Delevsky stood up. He was a tall man, and when he stood on his good leg, he seemed to tower over everyone, but when he brought his weight down on his maimed, shortened leg, he looked almost dwarf-like. 'That is Christ,' said Delevsky in ringing tones. 'Once again He is on His way to Jerusalem, poor, barefoot, half-naked and hungry, and none of you knew Him. No one even got up, no one spread his clothes on the floor for Him to warm His frozen feet. Ah, you!' he said, half mockingly, half disgustedly, came down on his lame leg and sat down again.

Soutine suddenly began to stammer with excitement. 'What do you think, would this stranger agree to pose for his portrait? What a face!'

Delevsky burst out laughing sardonically. 'That's it! That's exactly what we need—to immortalize the face of Christ! I'll certainly tell him the next time he comes.'

I do not know what came of Soutine's offer to paint the Jew's portrait; I do know that the offer of a pair of boots and a pair of trousers was refused.

'Isn't he the proud one!' said one of our group, and added cynically, 'He probably thinks he wouldn't get any alms if he were properly dressed.'

'Hold your tongue!' cried Delevsky. 'Your old boots and filthy trousers mean nothing to him, don't you understand? When he gets to Jerusalem he will be clothed there!'

The Jew appeared at the canteen once or twice more, and then vanished.

The second Russian canteen was run by the talented painter Marie Vassilieva, at one time known as '*la bonne a tout faire*', or 'Jack of all trades'. The canteen was in a courtyard off the avenue du Maine, next door to her studio, where she and her friends would work together on Negro-cubistic compositions. Everyone knew the tiny, bandy-legged woman, practically a dwarf, with her round, white, browless face, her thin mouth and small teeth. Everyone knew her piercing voice. Small people need their voice and character, for otherwise they are easily effaced by others; with her talent, mind and voice, no one could efface little Vassilieva.

The atmosphere in this canteen was quite different from Delevsky's. Here painters, writers and musicians would meet to discuss politics (this often ended in a fight), to argue over new art forms, to flirt and to dance to Zadkine's mad music, 'The Camel's Tango'. On Saturdays, after dinner, there were so-called serious concerts, and crowds of people came to sit on the tables, on the sideboards and on the floor. When Americans from the front wanted to see how artists lived, they would come to the canteen and give everyone gin mixed with vodka and whisky, and all hell would break loose.

The police, coming to investigate casualties and damage to furniture, would inevitably discover the hiding place of cases of wines and spirits. 'What's this?' a policeman would ask sternly.

'Can't you see? This is the only sure remedy for Spanish flu,' the little Vassilieva would reply with a smile.

The canteen would be closed down for a few days, but then, somehow, it would reopen. The pea soup with ham would be simmering again, the Russian chopped meat cutlets would be frying, and crowds of people would gather of an evening.

Modi was a favoured guest at Vassilieva's canteen, and of course she never charged him anything. Sometimes, when drunk, he would begin undressing under the eager eyes of the faded English and American girls who frequented the canteen. He would stand very erect and undo his girdle, which must have been four or five feet long, then let his trousers slip down to his ankles, then slowly pull his shirt up over his head and display himself quite naked, slim and white, his torso arched.

'Hi, look at me!' he would cry. 'Beautiful as a new-born babe or just out of the bath. Don't I look like a god?'

And he would start reciting verses. If they were not Dante, they were from *Les chants de Maldorer* by Lautréamont. Or perhaps he would sing in Italian. The words of his songs were not easy to understand, but one could make out frequent repetitions of '*Capelli biondi, vestita bianca*'.

The English and American girls would sigh, screw up their eyes and whisper, 'Ah, the beautiful Renaissance youth!'

Others were not so admiring. 'He's mad, and as drunk as a cab driver,' they would say.

Soutine, who often accompanied Modi (but seldom stayed long for fear of a fight), would always defend his friend. 'You can't say he's like a cab driver. He is a Renaissance youth. The environment doesn't suit him, that's the trouble.'

Another source of food for artists was Rosalie's *crémerie* in the rue Campagne Première. Like the Rotonde, like the canteens of Delevsky and Vassilieva, it was an institution in the Montparnasse of those days. What artist did not know this Neapolitan woman, who spent so much time struggling to make her customers pay? She was a fine woman, and in her restaurant one was at home. Numerous artists had reason to be grateful to her, particularly Modi, whom she adored, though she was frequently driven to fury by his drunkenness, his drug taking and his undisciplined behaviour.

Soutine told me that Rosalie, at one time a beauty, had enchanted some Russian prince in Naples and had had a child by him. This ardent love did not last; the prince vanished or died, and Rosalie was left with the child on her hands. When I knew him, the boy was about fourteen, thin, with skin of a magnificent brown, and very quiet. Frequently Rosalie abused him for his slowness in waiting at table or the like, calling him *asino, buricco*, and other less flattering Italian epithets, while he remained silent, glued to the wall, his hands hanging down, giving no sign of anger or defiance. We often scolded her for her impatient and brutal treatment of her son.

'But my God,' she defended herself, 'how I must have sinned before Him and Our Lady that they should have given me an ass! For he is an ass. If he is supposed to go forward, why, he backs up. He understands nothing and wants to do everything his own way—and so slowly. *Mamma mia*! If you sent him to fetch death itself, he would not bring it until there was no longer any need for it!'

Modi often stood up for the boy. 'If you are displeased with him, give him to me. He will be happy living with me.'

'What? What?' she would shriek. 'Give him to you? At fifteen he'll be a drunkard and a thief! Get out of here!' And she would take up her broom and sweep Modi out of the *crémerie*.

'*L'ignorante*,' Modi would say pityingly, 'so good but so stupid.'

Modi often came to Rosalie's with Soutine, whom she tolerated, having heard that he was a good painter, but did not really like, because he used to drink with Modi. Still, she was reluctant to take money from either of them. Sometimes she would refuse Modi's request for a bottle of wine, and then we all took cover (including Soutine), for Modi would fly into a fury, and everything in sight—glasses, plates, heavier objects—would be thrown.

Modi painted a fresco on one of the walls of the *crémerie*, but Rosalie did not like it. This made him angry. 'You are a fool,' he told her. 'Don't you realize that this fresco is worth 30,000 or 40,000 francs?'

Rosalie began to laugh. 'What? Is this filth worth so much money? Well, I don't want it.' And she shooed Modi out into the street.

The next day we were all horrified to see Rosalie's son covering the fresco with white paint.

When Modi died, Rosalie was greatly shaken. She wept and wept, telling anyone who would listen how sorry she was that she had not fed him better and perhaps helped him to live longer. She was sorry too about the fresco, which, she was informed, she could then have sold for between 300,000 and 500,000 francs.

* * *

It was at Rosalie's *crémerie* that I encountered for the first time an engaging giant of a man, courteous, prepossessing and an agreeable talker (his friends referred to him as 'the kindly cannibal'). This was the Mexican painter, Diego Rivera. He was not handsome, but he was impressive looking, and not only because of his size. His most striking features were his eyes, big, black and set aslant, and his nose, which was short and thick seen from the front, and aquiline in profile. His mouth was wide and sensual like Ehrenburg's, but with whiter, more even teeth. A small moustache covered his upper lip, giving him the look of a Saracen or a Moor, and he wore a beard, short and evenly trimmed, which fringed his chin in an oval. He had wide buttocks and flat feet, and his hands were small for his body. He dressed like a workman in blue dungarees stained with paint, as so many artists did; his enormous Mexican walking-stick and a wide-brimmed hat struck a more individual note. Rivera was generally accompanied by his wife in name, the Russian engraver, Angelina Beloff, and the sculptors, Lipchitz and Meschaninov, who were Russian too.

I soon formed the habit of visiting Rivera's studio in the rue du Départ, a habit shared by a good many others: Modi, Soutine, Picasso, Cocteau, Max Jacob, Apollinaire, Larionov, Gontcharova, Blanchard, Matisse, Juan Gris, Lhote, Friesz were some of those who came. We came to talk about painting, especially about cubism, construction and Cézanne, whose work Rivera had a passion for. Maintaining that Cubism had its origins in the teachings of this great French painter, Rivera would draw structural plans of Cézanne's pictures on a blackboard, to the fascination of us all. This was the heyday of Cubism and we were all interested in it. Modi became enthusiastic about Cubism for a time and painted several pictures under its influence (pictures that the public failed to understand but that his friends greatly admired). Matisse refused to accept the doctrines of Cubism and Futurism, but came because he wanted to understand Cézanne.

I listened avidly to these discussions. I also posed for Rivera and watched him at work. Under his influence, I learned to see nature and objects from a different angle, and my love of art became deeper and more complete. He also began to figure prominently in my social life. Little by little a circle of friends became defined and began to be seen together in various cafés and

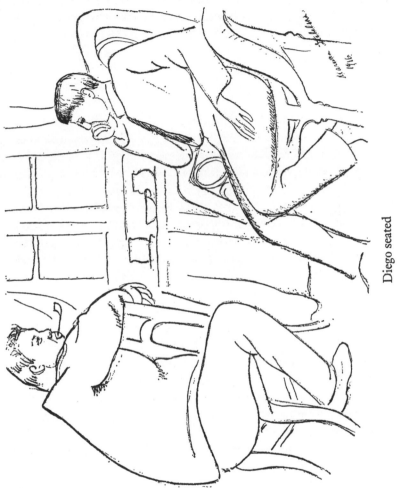

Diego seated

also at Poiret's in the rue du Faubourg St-Honoré, where exhibitions were organized: Rivera, Angelina (though she often stayed at home), Ehrenburg, Voloshin, Boris Savinkov (less frequently than the others), the sculptor Paul Cornet, Modigliani, Zadkine, Picasso and his wife and myself. Later on, our group was sometimes joined by Kisling, Léger, Apollinaire and the colourful Max Jacob.

* * *

Almost everything there is to say about Pablo Picasso has already been said and said again. This extraordinary painter has always been much talked of, often disparagingly: that is the price the great have to pay. I myself have always liked him as a painter and as a man. Nowadays his work commands astronomical prices, but Rivera once told me that when Picasso came to Paris from Barcelona he was extremely poor and used to carve and decorate pipes and sell them—for five francs apiece! Apollinaire and Max Jacob befriended him and played a great part in his artistic and spiritual development, but he owes the beginnings of his fame to the American art collector, Leo Stein, who bought Picasso's pictures (and Matisse's and Friesz's too) in 1912. This was during Picasso's blue period, inspired by El Greco—his best period, in my opinion.

I made Picasso's acquaintance early in the era of Cubism, *collages* and interest in Negro art. Before I met him, I used to see him with Max Jacob at the Rotonde or Rosalie's *crémerie* or on the boulevard Montparnasse, both looking as though they were in fancy dress. I took them for clowns or jockeys until I found out who they were and had a good laugh at my mistake. Picasso wore a long, ample checked coat, a big cap, and gaudy ties and scarves. He was rather short, but wiry and well-proportioned. His hair was very black with blue lights in it, and he was clean shaven. He had the profile of a Greek statue and a beautiful, voluptuous mouth. His eyes were very black and shone with the remarkable brilliance which they have retained to this day: I could realize his

66

presence in a crowd by his glance, which seemed literally to spring out of a mass of faces with an effect little short of hypnotic. Russians referred to him as '*le diabolique*,' which flattered him, I think. The fascination he has exerted over women throughout his life is well known.

I recall the day Voloshin, Ehrenburg, Katya, Savinkov and I decided to go and visit Picasso. If I remember rightly, he was then living opposite the Montparnasse cemetery, in the rue Froidevaux. We arrived at eleven o'clock. He opened the door wearing a blue-and-white striped bathing dress and a bowler hat. He made us look into each one of the numerous rooms, all of them arranged to serve as backgrounds for his still-lifes and portraits. We saw drawings and canvases everywhere, and piles of books cluttering up the tables and chairs. The floors were strewn with stained painting rags, cigarette ends and newspapers. On a big easel was a canvas, big, powerful, imaginative—and mysterious. No one wished to risk asking what it represented, for fear of blundering. There we stood, respectful, silent, stupefied. It was Voloshin, finally, unable to restrain a poet's curiosity, who asked what the picture represented.

'Oh, nothing much, you know,' Picasso answered, smiling. 'Between ourselves, it's some dung. Good for idiots.'

'Thank you, thank you,' said Voloshin and Ehrenburg.

'Don't think I meant that for you, *chers messieurs*. You're different. But I often have to work for fools who are ignorant about art, and my dealer is always asking me to do something to astonish the public.'

Was Picasso being sincere? He was not very sociable that day. Perhaps our visit was keeping him from abandoning himself, in his astonishing bathing dress, to a spell of swimming in his bathroom. He saw us to the door as nicely and pleasantly as possible. Later on, when I knew him better, he half-jokingly invited me to come one day and have a bathe at his house. 'Only give me notice because my bathroom is always dirty.'

* * *

Like Picasso, Max Jacob had a remarkable glance, full of slyness and irony, sweetness and gaiety. His face was distinctive, with its shining shaven skull, big nose, wide, sensual mouth and long, pointed chin like Punch himself. Though small of stature, Jacob had a stately bearing and a touch of the grand manner. He dressed flamboyantly, in early years affecting a black cloak and a black bowler and later on a well-cut grey greatcoat, ties of a different colour for every day of the week, white gloves, spats, a top hat and an eyeglass. But one could sense the sadness and anguish under this music-hall dandyism. When he began to age, he used to powder himself in the evenings to conceal the ravages of time and soften his features.

I often wondered: who was the real Max Jacob? Was it the one who was nice, obliging, gentle and rather shy? Or the one who rattled away like a light woman, cursing his friends and railing at his enemies, wordly, biting and ironical? His nature was very unbalanced. Sometimes it was impossible to talk seriously to him, for he would skilfully change the subject or give nonsensical answers or make fun of everybody and everything (his improvised parodies on himself and his friends were very funny indeed). Sometimes he could be wonderfully sympathetic. I remember that shortly after my father's suicide he asked me why I was so sad and kept so much to myself, and I poured out everything—my prophetic childhood dreams about my father's death, my uncle's accusations, my feelings of guilt. He heard me out with genuine concern.

Max Jacob was the son of a Jewish antiquarian bookseller in Brittany. He had a strong mystical bent, encompassing the subtlety of a Cabbalist, illuminist, Talmudist and astrologer and the naïveté of a Breton peasant. At the end of his *Art poétique* he wrote, 'I dreamed of re-creating earthly life in the atmosphere of heaven', and these words explain all his poetry. One of his most important works is *Poèmes en prose*, it is directed against soulless 'literary' poetry and is enthroned under the name of 'Surrealism' launched by Apollinaire. In his prose works Max Jacob was a moralist, depicting the misery of man without God.

Like his good friend Modigliani, Jacob led a dissolute life; this caused him untold torment, and he was haunted by an intense fear of hell. He became a convert to Catholicism and was baptized, with Picasso standing godfather, in Notre Dame de Sion on 10 February, 1914, receiving the name of Cyprian. This did not bring any immediate change in his habits, for soon afterwards I saw him at Kisling's studio lying on the floor with a handsome boy and behaving lasciviously. 'He's cracked, you know,' Kisling said to me, with a laugh. 'He's turned Catholic, but look how he acts, the swine. And yet, if I asked him for his best coat, he'd give it to me for nothing. He takes drugs, you know. He says he saw Christ in his room, very handsome and smart. Sounds likely! If I were Christ I wouldn't go into Max's room, never fear.' I felt a deep sense of shame for Jacob—and for Kisling.

In 1921, claiming that in Paris he sinned all the time because people bothered and irritated him, Max Jacob began going to St Benoît-sur-Loire, seeking solitude in order to come closer to God. But he was unable (or unwilling) to abandon the world, and there followed a period of restless travel, full of foppery and dissipation. Finally, overcome with self-disgust, he returned to St Benoît-sur-Loire for good. I should like to think that he found tranquillity in his last days. There comes a moment in life when one sees distinctly what to avoid, what can only disfigure and enfeeble soul and mind. Max Jacob saw, and tried to escape from his private hell into the refuge of quietness and rectitude. I should like to think he succeeded.

On 27 February, 1944, Max Jacob was taken by the Germans to the camp at Drancy. There he fell ill and died. He is buried at Ivry.

* * *

When Fernand Léger was called up and his wife Jeanne, who was amiable, amusing, and pretty, remained in Paris, I used to spend joyful, uproarious evenings with her at her husband's studio. But one evening with her struck a very different note, and turned out badly for me. One of her best friends, a Polish sculptress, had died suddenly. She had been an extremely fascinating woman, gifted with great sex appeal, had led a fast life and had had quite a fling—so much of one that it had often been predicted that she would sooner or later end up in hospital. A few of us went with the funeral procession to Montrouge cemetery and came back late in the evening, chilled and saddened by the ceremony, to Jeanne's, where we drank wine and comforted her. All of us were thinking of ourselves or of those near and dear to us (my thoughts were of my father, who had now been dead for a year). When I left the studio I climbed up on a bench in the boulevard Montparnasse and perched on the back like a bird. I suffered a giddy spell, the effect of the wine and the fatigue of the day, and fell backwards, landing on my head. It did not seem to be much of a disaster—simply a bump that soon stopped hurting.

But after some days my eyes began to swell shut. I ran to the hospital, where my urine and a sample of my blood were analysed to determine the cause of my malady, without result. I went home, but the condition got worse. The next day I could hardly discern my face in the glass, for my eyes were almost closed; also, my face was misshapen and I looked like an old Eskimo woman. I could not go out with a face like that. Thereupon I got into bed, saying to myself, 'You've done heaps of stupid things. You've wasted heaps of precious time instead of working. Well done. The foolish vanity of a pretty girl, laziness, heedlessness—that's all finished, quite finished. There's nothing left but to wait for the inevitable. A sad end, but you've earned it.'

For two days I stayed in bed, my eyes shut, in absolute darkness, measuring time by the noises of the school children going to school, coming back for lunch, setting off again, and coming home in the evening. I was plagued by hunger and very cold. No one came to see me, not even my concierge.

On the second evening, I heard footsteps on the stairs. Someone knocked at the door, which was not locked, and came in. It was Jeanne.

'Well, my dear, what are you doing in the dark? No response?

70

Have you been struck dumb?'

She lit the lamp, took a look at me and cried out, 'But how frightful! What's happened to you, my poor girl? Listen, I'm going to fetch a taxi. We'll collect some of your things and I'll take you to my place. Everyone's been asking where you've got to, and to think that you were here all alone and ill!'

She ran for a taxi, helped me downstairs and put me into it, but before leaving she insisted on going to see the concierge who had left me all alone like that, only to find the poor woman in bed with influenza.

'Your shanty seems rather unlucky,' commented Jeanne.

When she had put me to bed in her studio, made tea and prepared something for me to eat, she went out to the Rotonde to inform my friends and to look for a Danish doctor, a lover of the arts, who drank like a fish but cared for sick artists for nothing with a rare devotion. He came at once, as usual rather drunk. He examined me carefully, affirmed that my state was the result of a shock, and wrote a prescription. Jeanne raced off to the chemist and brought back ointments and bottles of medicine and lotions for bathing my eyes, as well as bandages to protect them from the light. Bandaged, I looked as if I had been badly wounded, and for several days I had to endure total blindness, during which time Max Voloshin, Ehrenburg and Katya, Rivera and Cornet and numerous others filed past me. It would all have been funny, if it had not been so very sad.

'It's strange to see you with half a face,' said Voloshin. 'It isn't Marevna any more—it's a nameless being. Only your mouth still tells me it's you.'

At this, the Danish doctor kissed me on the lips. I recoiled.

'Oh, you little devil,' said the doctor with a laugh. 'The wild girl that one could never get near! We'll be able to profit from this now.'

Voloshin came to sit beside me and put his arms around me. 'Now, now,' he said, 'don't hurt her. I know that she's already repenting of many things, and as soon as she's well everything will be different, won't it?'

71

I felt tears stinging my eyes. It was true. I swore to myself and promised my friends that in future I would be good.

Suddenly Cornet started singing in a voice that was slightly raucous:

> *Au café d'la Rotonde*
> *Une petite Marevna il y avait*
> *Qui chantait tous les jours*
> *Qu'elle allait s'en aller ;*
> *Et puis elle est tombée,*
> *Ell' s'est cassée la tête,*
> *Ell' s'est fait mal aux yeux,*
> *Pauv' petit' Marevna !*
> *Pauv' petit' Marevna !*

Everybody laughed, and Jeanne, seeing I was tired, sent them away. The doctor assured me he would come back next day—to kiss me on the mouth, he added with a laugh. I heard Voloshin murmur to Jeanne that he would return next day too to bring her money to pay for what I was costing her. I felt enormously fortunate in having such good friends.

For several days more, I still could see nothing. I suffered, but I knew that my accident was doing me good: it gave me a chance to plumb the depths, the darkness of my being. Little by little, the swelling went down and my sight returned to normal.

On my last day with Jeanne, there was a knock at the door. Jeanne went to open it, and I heard her exclaim, then give way to a fit of giggling. In a moment she returned. Ehrenburg was with her. A transformed Ehrenburg. Gone was the shoulder-length cascade of hair. His skull was bald and pale, and his head looked more like a horse's than ever. I began to giggle too, though of course it was not at all funny. For some time now Ehrenburg had been drinking too much—much too much. Perhaps this was an inevitable result of the way he was driving himself. He spent many strenuous nights hauling packing-cases at the station. Sometimes he disappeared for days at a time, having gone to the front under the aegis of the Red Cross or on a 'revictualling' errand. Upon his return, he would set to work on his article. Often he did not sleep all night.

He would sit up very late writing, then go straight out and knock about the streets. In the morning he would turn up at the Rotonde, grey in the face and exhausted, and resume writing. He began to behave a little crazily. At the café, in the street, at Jeanne's, he would utter strident shouts. We never could be sure whether he was joking or in the grip of some kind of *delirium tremens*.

In the face of our laughter, Ehrenburg became belligerent and almost frantic. 'I believe I'm going mad,' he said, and told us how early that morning he had been picked up wandering the streets by the police and sent to Charenton, where they had shaved his head and subjected him to a humiliating examination before letting him go. 'Tell me the truth, Jeanne—and you too, Marevna,' he begged. 'Am I really going mad or not?'

We hastened to reassure him. Jeanne made some good, strong coffee and we drank it together. I was deeply saddened by the change in Ehrenburg, but I told myself that we were all changing under the stress of wartime. Shortly afterwards, Ehrenburg left for the south with Katya and their little daughter in an effort to get his health back.

As soon as I regained my looks, my friends held a gathering to celebrate my recovery. And celebrate we did. There might have been the war, with its tensions, separations, and permanent blanks, but we who had escaped it so far made haste to take great mouthfuls of the life that was menaced day by day. I set to work again with enthusiasm.

* * *

One evening I went to the Salon des Indépendants and saw Rivera's painting, 'La Vierge Enceinte' which mystified me. Then I met Rivera somewhere, and he said he was glad to see my face again. We talked of his painting and I went to his studio to see some canvases. My visit made me thoughtful. I liked his painting very much and was deeply moved by it. But it was not only the paintings that accounted for my state of mind. While I was at his studio, I was struck by how Angelina spoke to this great giant as though he were a small boy, calling him '*muchachito*', '*detochka*', '*bébé*', and how he talked similarly to her. They seemed very closely united and very happy.

I left them promising myself to see Rivera again as little as possible. I was always rather frightened of him. When I encountered him in the street I ran like a rabbit to the opposite pavement and pretended not to see him (a trick that exasperated him). Had I a presentiment that he would influence me greatly and turn my whole life upside down? It is strange that I wanted to avoid this big, unusual man, but felt myself oddly drawn towards him at the same time.

Suddenly, I fell ill again. I could not eat: hardly would I swallow a bite, when I was in such agony that I had to lie down. One doctor advised one thing, another the opposite. I felt desperate. Then came a letter from the Ehrenburgs, urging me to take the train at once and come to them at Èze, near Nice. Money was enclosed. I felt a great surge of gratitude and set off almost at once, after saying *au revoir* to Rivera with very mixed feelings.

I found Ilya looking rested and hirsute and almost like his old self. 'I won money at the casino at Monte Carlo,' he said. 'So you see, we didn't forget you, Marevna.'

I felt happy to be with these good friends again. In their pink villa on the hill, a fine dinner awaited me—lobster, all kinds of *zakuski* and an impressive array of bottles. But I could not touch a single one of the delicacies, nor drink either.

Next day the Ehrenburg's friend Tikhon, another journalist, took me to Nice to see Dr Rosanov, a kindly, bearded man, said to be the best doctor in the town. He began by complimenting me on my body, remarking that it was always pleasant to have a pretty girl for a patient. Then he prescribed a perfectly simple regimen. I was to begin sunbathing, ten minutes every morning, uncovering myself little by little and increasing the time of exposure until I could stand half an hour naked—the maximum. He also prescribed Belloc's charcoal, milk of magnesia and avoiding tinned food.

'You'll see,' he promised, 'In a week you'll be fit again, and

74

you'll come to see me and taste one of my fine wines. That will do you the greatest good.'

I was indeed cured, thanks, I really believe, to the sunbathing and to a simple, healthy diet (since then I have always taken sunbaths and eaten quantities of yoghurt). But I did not go back to see the good doctor, even to thank him, for I was wary of his fine wine and his fine beard. Once, at Tiflis, a gypsy had foretold that a bearded man would wreck my life, and ever since I had mistrusted bearded men.

The days I spent at Èze were joyous ones. Our villa was hidden among pink rose-trees and surrounded by olives with, here and there, a black cypress. The cicadas, maddened by the intoxicating scents and by the heat of the summer sun, sang from morning to night. When darkness fell, the crickets began their monotonous tune, which I have always loved, and hundreds of glow-worms gleamed with their phosphorescent green and gave their mysterious signals in the thickets. The sea summoned me early in the morning, a time I adored swimming; also after sunset, when the water was warm and still. I looked down into the transparent waters and envied the fish that fled from my shadow. I envied the sea-wreck so mysteriously sunk in the depths. I even envied the crabs with their ridiculous gait and teased them with my foot. I was filled with a mad glee and sang and shouted at the top of my voice. I wanted to be a fish, a swallow that grazes the surface of the water with its wing. On my return to the villa, I felt wholly renewed and purified by the water: at those moments I loved life and all the world.

'It's amazing how you change, Marevna,' Ehrenburg said. 'One might think you really were a sea nymph.'

It was the sun, the sea, the song of the cicadas, above all the blessed friendship I was offered that worked the miracle. I regained my health and my poise. I began to work, painting several cubist pictures.

The time at Èze was full, apart from work. We took turns to do the cooking. For a whole week one person had to prepare the midday meals for five critical people, which was no joke. Ehrenburg was the severest critic. He was also the worst cook. Faced with some of his meals, we had no choice but to flee down to the beach where there was an inexpensive little *bistro*. Sometimes we went to Nice to see Boris Savinkov and his wife Marusya, whom he had married to discharge a debt of honour (her brother, an officer, had taken Boris's place in his cell after Boris had been condemned to death). Sometimes we climbed to the top of the hill on which the old village of Èze is perched. There we had a marvellous view of the entire bay of Nice and Monte Carlo. Èze, seen from a distance, resembled a corsairs' lair, but its old churches, its ramparts, its narrow alleys full of shadow, and its ambling people gave us a feeling of serenity. We would descend towards sunset to rejoin Ehrenburg at the villa, for his heart would not permit him to climb so high.

He did bathe, though. Or rather, he went to the edge of the water, wet his feet and hands and then remained pensively warming himself in the sun, exposing his white body all covered with black hairs, like an orang-outang's. I could not help laughing when I looked at him from a distance—he really justified the nickname of 'the sloth' that one of our friends had bestowed on him.

Ridiculous as he looked, no one was in any doubt as to his sex. The case was otherwise with me. Once some gendarmes saw me bathing naked, but from too far away to tell whether I was a man or a woman. The next day two of them came to the villa and asked about me. Surely, if I were naked, they could tell, Ilya said. Oh, they hadn't been as close as that. Then, if they couldn't tell, where was the harm? Forbidden. Papers! Alas, I had no papers. In my scatterbrained way, I had left them in Paris. I sent for them, and a few days later my sex was officially established by the gendarmerie.

In the evenings, after putting the child to bed, Ehrenburg, Tikhon and Katya started drinking 'till the soul left the body', as Katya put it. Relations among the three were strained, for Katya had fallen in love with Tikhon, who was not brilliant like Ilya, but gentle and good, and a friend one could count on. Years of coping with the capricious, exigent, selfish temperament of genius had wearied her, and the time came when she could no longer share

Ehrenburg's bed. Later on, she married Tikhon in Russia and had several children by him. In spite of the triangle, the three remained good friends.

During my stay at Èze I received two letters from Rivera, whom Ehrenburg kept referring to as '*ton* Mexicain,' '*ton* sauvage'. This infuriated me, though at the same time I was pleased. In the letters, cryptically, Rivera expressed his fondness for me, but I refused to take this seriously. I reminded myself that he was married and I resolved: 'That man isn't for me'.

* * *

But back in Paris I began to see more and more of Rivera, though I made a point of never going to his studio or his apartment by myself. Now and again, when he saw that I had no money, he would slip me a fifteen- or a twenty-franc note. (He was not the only one either: other friends, particularly Yura, Gorki's stepson, also prevented me from falling into black destitution, and I am most warmly grateful to them all.) I felt keenly how very much alone I was, surrounded by those artists who all, with the exception of Voloshin, had some kind of intimate relationship. Naturally a good many requests were made to me, but I always shunned them. Angelina often asked me why I didn't become engaged to the sculptor Meschaninov, a short, broad man with a round, red face, rather conceited, who paid court to me.

Rivera urged me to accept him. 'He's a very good chap. He'd be an excellent friend to you, you know, and he's very fond of you.'

Unfortunately, I liked neither Meschaninov nor his sculpture, but I was often teased about him none the less. Sometimes at Rivera's, I would get fed up with it and take refuge under the table. Then Rivera would crawl under the cloth on all fours to join me, and we would stay there, talking innocently, until Angelina lifted the cloth and handed us a lighted candle, saying, 'In darkness one can't see what one's doing properly'. Everyone would roar with laughter, and Rivera and I would emerge from our hiding place, smiling.

77

Rivera was a veritable child—erratic, spoiled, sensitive, excitable. Yet when I looked round me, out of all those men (omitting Picasso, who was handsome and stood out from the rest) it was Rivera I liked most, in spite of his flat feet, his great belly and his slovenly dress. I was fascinated by his superb Saracen's head, the prominent eyes that sometimes seemed to burst into flame, the way he had of turning pale and then red. When he opened his mouth to speak everybody listened, not only because of what he said but because of the way he said it.

He had one very disturbing trait—fits of what might be called 'lunacy'. I remember, vividly, the first time I witnessed one of these fits. He suddenly stopped talking and turned white; his face was motionless, his eyes showing only the whites. Everyone fell silent and watched him. He rose up with his great Mexican stick (wherever it was, he always found it at these moments) and went to the door. Angelina tried to stop him by talking to him gently, but he put her aside, opened the door and went down the completely darkened stairs to the street. Everyone followed him—at a distance. I was distressed at this spectacle; I had never seen anything like it. I wanted to say good-bye to my friends and return to my studio, but Rivera would not let me go. He accompanied me home and declared that he would allow no one to enter my door. I was very glad to find myself alone, and I did not go near him for several days.

Angelina explained to me that at such moments he must not be thwarted, but treated very gently. Then one might sometimes manage to persuade him to go to bed. She told me that he suffered from these fits regularly, and the more tired he was the oftener they recurred. They were probably due to his liver, she said, which was in a very bad state.

And now, in addition to my admiration for the artist, pity was growing in me for the man. I began to realize that he required as much care and attention as a child, and I felt pity for Angelina too, since I knew that for ten years she had lived and coped with his condition. (I have noticed that in general men put up with illness very badly, while women, condemned to the discomforts which start at puberty, are capable of greater stoicism and patience.)

Angelina talked to me of Rivera's weakness for women, laughing as she said, 'I'm not really afraid of these women. They're usually very stupid—flirts who like to see every man at their feet. He very soon tires of them. I shut my eyes and he always comes back to me at the end.' Did she mean that as a warning to me?

One evening, when I had a cold, Ehrenburg, Picasso and I went to Rivera's studio, and I spent the time (which went very quickly) making sketches of Rivera sitting astride his chair and of Picasso in an armchair by the table.

When it was time for us to go, Rivera said, 'Marevnochka has a very bad cold. I know there's no fire in her studio. She'd much better stay here. She can sleep behind the screen.'

Ehrenburg and Picasso went off by themselves and I remained. Rivera and Angelina made up a fine, clean bed for me on the sofa and put up the screen. I went right to sleep, but I was suddenly awakened by voices on the other side of the screen. It seemed to me, in the echoing darkness of the huge studio, that I was hearing a dialogue between persons I did not know, not Rivera and Angelina. Someone was mourning in a mixture of Spanish, French and Russian, while someone else murmured soothingly. I realized that Rivera was trying to leave their bed and that Angelina was trying to restrain him and placate him.

'I love Marevna,' I heard. 'I love her and I can't help it. It's you who must tell her. I shall never be able to.'

'Yes, yes,' was the rejoinder. 'Don't be uneasy, she shall be told. But now go to sleep or you'll wake her up and she'll be alarmed. Sleep, *muchachito.* . . .'

My heart was throbbing in my chest. Was he joking in order to test me? Was I listening to the rambling of delirium?

In the morning I wanted to go away, but they would not hear of it. I had a headache, my ears hurt and I was shivering. It was clear that I had influenza. They put me in the back room, and hardly had I got into bed when I began twitching about like a fish in a frying pan, devoured by fever. The stove was set alight, and it smoked like a factory chimney. I coughed and wept and felt I

79

would suffocate. When the window was opened to make a through draft, Rivera wrapped me in blankets and carried me in his arms to the studio.

'We must wait till the smoke goes away,' he said. 'We must be careful not to let you fall really ill, Marevnochka. You are going to stay here until you get well.'

I said nothing. Each word of his went straight to my heart, In the giddiness of fever I felt very happy, gathered in the arms of this giant, this 'kindly cannibal'. At that moment I cared for nothing. I was doing nothing wrong. I was ill. I was loved. Someone was sorry for lonely, fragile Marevna, lost in the icy wilderness of Paris without an ounce of coal because of the war that went on and on and made everybody suffer.

I spent several days in bed in the back room. Angelina was a kind and attentive nurse. In the evenings, Rivera came and sat on the edge of my bed and looked at me. The nights were virtual repetitions of the first. I thought Angelina must surely be hurt by Rivera's incoherent talk, which consisted of admission after admission. She would ask me every morning whether I had slept well and whether I had heard anything—Diego had had a mild attack. I always assured her that I had been much too feverish to hear anything but the buzzing in my ears.

I left as soon as I had recovered, vowing to see Rivera as little as possible. While I was ill Angelina had confessed to me that she was pregnant—a good reason for my avoiding the studio in the rue de Départ. I felt a void in my life. I had acquired a taste for the visits to Rivera and Angelina; I enjoyed the atmosphere of work and peace around them.

I worked in my icy studio. The monthly supply of coal allotted to artists by the government (fifty kilogrammes) arrived and soon vanished, for the studio was vast and the walls were almost entirely of glass. I saw much of my friends, and they helped to drive depression away.

Voloshin, Savinkov, Ehrenburg and I attended a gay and lively evening at the S's. The handsome Leonide Massine was there and the brilliant Max Jacob. And of course Rivera. He drew me into

Apollinaire, Max Jacob, Cocteau

an empty room and into a goblet of champagne mingled drops of
our blood: an Indian rite, he said, which would bind us together
for years, for eternity. We emptied the goblet, gazing into each
other's eyes. Was it a joke or a real charm?

As our lips met over the goblet, Voloshin came in, and saying
with a laugh that he had never drunk blood except when he had
sucked a cut on his finger, insisted on drinking some Mexican
blood mixed with his own Russo-German. The rite was repeated,
and suddenly we all fell silent, perhaps under a spell cast by
Rivera, sorcerer or priest. Back in the drawing room we refused to
say what we had been doing. Everybody noticed that we looked

quite blissful. They noticed too that Diego, Voloshin and I now addressed each other as '*tu*'.

'They've obviously drunk a love philtre,' said Ehrenburg.

Angelina began going out less and less. She was thirty-five, some years older than Rivera and twelve years my senior, and her first pregnancy, coming late, caused her much suffering. But Diego would come out in the evening with the rest of us, to a café or perhaps to the Russian ballet, which he was mad about. I found myself caught up in a dangerous game and, instead of avoiding Rivera, I allowed myself to come closer and closer to the man who both frightened and fascinated me.

Although there was nothing between us yet, all Montparnasse was talking of our affair, criticizing us and pitying Angelina. My friends teased me unmercifully.

'He's ugly, Rivera,' they said, 'and dirty.'

'No more than Ehrenburg,' I retorted.

Once, when Marcel Rivière, in an issue of the *Cri de Paris*, had referred to Ehrenburg as 'this dirty, lousy Jewish poet who calls himself a Russian', I went to the Dôme to find the journalist and squirt his face with a siphon—'for the lousy Jew'. That did not stop me doing the same to Ilya when he spoke to me of 'your questionable Mexican'.

Boris Savinkov, on the eve of a journey to Russia, invited Rivera and me to dinner in a restaurant and watched us with his sly, narrow, glittering eyes. 'I shall soon be returning to Paris,' he said, 'and I hope to find you married, Marevna, and wearing lovely long frocks and hats and jewels. Would you like to have children?'

And again, as we were parting: 'Go on being good. Go on being the delicious child you are today. But stop whistling in the street and don't trust cannibals, even kindly ones.'

Rivera sometimes paid me surprise visits when I was working in my studio, giving me very good advice and talking to me of classical and modern painting. He showed some of my cubist pictures to Matisse, who thought them very interesting. He also introduced me to Paul Rosenberg, with whom he was about to sign a contract. It was very cold that day, and there was no fire in my studio; I was wearing a cloak and a *bashlyk* (Caucasian fur hood) on my head. Rosenberg was struck by the look of my studio, which was very long, with a low ceiling—and also, perhaps, by the sight of me. He bought two canvases, and Rivera confided to me that I might possibly be offered a contract. Unfortunately, they parted soon afterwards, and nothing came of it.

Sometimes Rivera and I went to the Louvre or to exhibitions or to see artists we knew. Or he would take me home with him, where Angelina was altering her old frocks and preparing baby linen.

Angelina was often nervy and irritable. Once, when Rivera balked at the idea of accompanying her somewhere, she railed at him, on the verge of tears. 'You're always willing to go out with other people. You never have to be asked twice! But you don't care to go out with me any more!'

Of course her condition was largely responsible for the outburst, but the charge was not completely without foundation. I often said to Rivera, 'Go and stay with your wife. It's not right to leave her alone so much.'

'It's not my fault that she's pregnant,' he would say. 'It wasn't I who wanted a child.'

This answer was so childish, so typically masculine, and it annoyed me. Had it not taken two of them to make a child? I have since come to understand that men always say that when they want to evade their responsibilities to the woman and the child—if they do not go even further and say that the child is not theirs.

About this time Max Voloshin prepared to join his mother in the Crimea and asked me to go with him. Picasso urged me to remain in Paris, where they would make an artist of me, greater than Marie Laurencin. Rivera said nothing: he merely looked at me.

I refused Voloshin's invitation, and Rivera and I saw him off.

'I entrust her to you, Diego,' Voloshin said solemnly, 'We are brothers by the blood we drank together. She is your sister. Promise to protect her from harm.'

Rivera promised.

* * *

83

One morning Ehrenburg turned up at my door, all tousled and trembling. 'Listen, Marevna! Last night Diego came to my hotel stark raving. It's a wonder he didn't try to kill me. He whirled his Mexican stick round my head shouting that he wanted you at any price—I swear he's losing his wits. What is there between you?'

I assured him that there was nothing, that it was one of Diego's usual fits and would go as it had come.

'No, you idiot. It can't possibly pass off like that. Here. Here's the letter he left for me. Read it and you'll see what's up.'

It was a long letter. I scanned it quickly.

Dear Ilya,

I love Marevna and Angelina knows. I've told her several times. My life is a burden to me now. I can't stand living with my wife any longer—she's not really my wife, anyhow. The child she is expecting is a misfortune that I never wished for. She did it on purpose in order to keep me. But I don't love her any more. I have a great affection for her, for she has always been a good friend to me, but that's all. Talk to Marevna. This can't go on. She must go away, or she must stay here and belong to me. . . . Angelina agrees to our separating.

There was much more, all of it in the same vein.

'You see what you've done?' said Ilya.

'I? I've done nothing at all. I've done everything I could to prevent its coming to this. I like him very much, but. . . . Just when his wife's expecting a baby? Monstrous! I'm beginning to believe he is mad, as you say. Or perhaps he just needs a woman, since he can't make love to his wife. It wouldn't take him long to find one. He's only got to look.'

'No, no! Listen, Marevna. Don't you want to experience a great love? You, who are so romantic and so fastidious about men? Well, here is your opportunity—a grand adventure. All you need is the courage to live it.'

'What will be the end of it?'

'How do you expect me to answer that? It depends on so many things. But make up your mind quickly. I wouldn't spend another night like that for anything. Even if he doesn't knock me on the

84

head I shall go mad too. Be brave, Marevna. One doesn't often have the chance of such a love. And to tell the truth,' he added with an ironical smile, 'your Diego hasn't such bad taste.'

He left me the letter and I lay down on my bed, considering seriously, honestly, whether I wanted love from Rivera. Could I believe in his feeling for me? He had not spoken to me himself, but very likely he could not have found words to convince me of his devotion. I knew he was fond of me and interested in my work. Of course I wanted him to like me, but I had made no effort to attract him. Nothing could have been simpler than the way I dressed, in a pair of hand-woven pyjamas (a present from Foujita), with the trousers rolled so as not to show under my overcoat, and the *bashlyk* on my head. But I was gay, impulsive, lively, shy (though sometimes audacious), a good comrade, obliging and at the same time proud and plain-spoken. Doubtless this mixture had its charm, when reinforced by youth and the desire to be happy and make others so.

Could I make him happy? I felt strangely drawn towards this odd man in whom were united the power of genius and the weakness of a child. But I did not know whether I loved him as Angelina did, with the same self-abnegation and patience. I still felt an aversion for physical possession. Passion, as I knew from my first reversal, was transitory; what I wanted was tenderness and affection. To tell the truth I was too young, and the word 'love' still had for me a halo of poetry. To look at, there was nothing poetic about Rivera, apart from his face. He neglected himself, cared little how he looked, often had a dirty neck, and emitted a smell peculiar to fat people. While our relationship was still only that of friends he often took me on to his knees, and I breathed in the odour of his hair and beard, of his chest too—a mixture of musk, turpentine and linseed oil—and I did not find this unpleasant. But mingled with it was another odour, which repelled me and took away all the pleasure of staying in that position. (Men must sometimes avoid a woman because of too strong a smell. Love may tolerate this kind of thing, but desire, I believe, cannot endure it.)

And then there was the baby—a cruel problem. Angelina, whose position had never been legalized, would be deeply wounded if she saw herself threatened with abandonment at the very moment when she should feel herself bound more closely than ever to her child's father. And myself? It was as though I had defrauded her of Diego, profited by her kindness, in a sense betrayed the friendship and love of both of them.

What was I to say to Diego, then, if he came to talk to me about his being in love? I decided to be honest and sincere—if possible.

Towards evening I heard his heavy step on the stair. As soon as I opened the door I was struck by his distorted, tormented face, his feverish, mournful eyes. He put down his hat and his great stick and sat on my bed, gazing at me in silence.

'Are you ill?' I asked him. 'Or annoyed by something?'

'Annoyed is the word,' he replied. 'I'm sick of Rosenberg and his demands. He wants a contract with me, but he's not offering enough money and he's asking for too many pictures.'

I pointed out to him that a contract would be a sure way of getting him launched, since it was always to the interest of every dealer to puff his nurslings. 'Look at Picasso and the speed of his rise,' I concluded.

'I've no desire to work. I'm disgusted with everything. There's something missing. Impetus—something.'

It was painful to look at him. I should have liked to give him an innocent, affectionate kiss as usual, but I knew that I should only risk being caught up in other feelings. I had to go on struggling, resisting, for my own sake and for his. I told myself that if he went away without saying anything, I should not breathe a word about Ehrenburg's call.

All of a sudden he caught sight of the letter, which I had inadvertently left on the table, snatched it up, crumpled it and stuffed it in his pocket.

'Ilya's been to see you, then? He's spoken to you? You've nothing to say?'

'Listen, Diego, do you think it's very honourable of us to play at love when from one day to another your wife is expecting a

86

Michel Kikoine   Self-portrait (The Wounded Hunter), 1929
Oil on canvas—81 x 54 cm *(approx.* 32 x 21 inches)

2　**Marevna**　Portrait of Kisling
Oil on canvas—130 x 89.5 cm (*approx.* 51 x 35 inches)

Mané Katz   *Wandering musicians,* 1927
Oil on canvas—81 x 73 cm (*approx. 32 x 29 inches*)

4 **Marevna**   Portrait of Mané Katz
Oil on canvas—97 x 130.5 cm (*approx.* 38 x 51 inches)

Marevna Homage to Diaghilev and to the friends of the Train Bleu
(Gontcharova, Larionev, Cocteau, Diaghilev, Stravinsky,
Picasso)
Oil on canvas—199 x 209.5 cm (*approx.* 78 x 82 inches)

6   **Marevna**   Homage to the friends of Montparnasse (Diego Rivera, Ehrenburg, Picasso, Chagall and Fernand Léger)
Oil on canvas—160 x 305 cm (*approx*. 63 x 120 inches)

Marevna Two women weeping, 1954
Oil on canvas—91.5 x 73.5 cm (*approx.* 36 x 29 inches)

8   **Diego M. Rivera**   Portrait of the Dutch sculptor, Fisher, 1918
Drawing—16 x 13 cm (*approx.* 6 x 5 inches)

Marevna *Top*: Green landscape *Oil on canvas*
Left: Old Provençal peasant man *Oil on canvas*
Right: Old Provençal peasant woman *Oil on canvas*

10 **Marevna**   Marika nude with Persian rug, 1946
Oil on canvas—81 x 99 cm (*approx.* 32 x 39 inches)

Chaim Soutine   Carcass of an ox, 1923
Oil on canvas—18 x 50.5 cm (*approx.* 7 x 20 inches)

12   **Marevna**   Portrait of Soutine
       Oil on canvas—66.5 x 51 cm (*approx.* 26 x 20 inches)

Chaim Soutine   *Top*: Woman bathing, *c.* 1927   *Oil on canvas*
Bottom: Windy day, Auxerre, 1939   *Oil on canvas*

14 **Chaim Soutine** House at Oisème, 1934
Oil on canvas—65.5 x 67.5 cm (*approx.* 26 x 27
inches)

Chaim Soutine   Hanging turkey, *c.* 1926
Oil on canvas—91.5 x 72.5 cm (*approx.* 36 x 29
inches)

16   **Marc Chagall**   En route (Wandering Jew), 1924
Oil on canvas—72 x 57 cm (*approx.* 28 x 22 inches)

baby—a child of *yours*? I don't feel very comfortable about it. My conscience tells me that it would be heartless to strike her such a blow at the very moment when she needs you most. Later on, perhaps.'

'She has all my friendship and affection, but it is you I love, Marevna. And she knows that now—I've told her everything. I've been fighting against myself for a long time, but I can't go on. If you had gone to Russia, I should have left here too. If I let myself be tied down by Paul Rosenberg it's in order to secure myself a position in the world—it's for her and for you, because I want to help both of you. But I must be free in my private life. I told Angelina I want to be free to live with you. Do you want me?'

'Remember Max's words? "Protect her from harm". But here you are, trying to drag me into an adventure that neither of us can see the end of.'

'Don't think that, Marevna. I'm not a cad or a gigolo. Would you like to see my papers? You'll see that I'm a nobleman. I have a title. My father and grandfather were grandees of Spain.'

'I'm not interested in that. Where would it lead us?'

'What are you interested in, then? I'm not rich, but that will come, you'll see. If I offer you my love sincerely, honourably, it's because—for a long time I've kept nothing from Angelina—I believe you love me too. Would you like me to marry you to-morrow? Nothing easier.'

Did he really think I would answer, 'All right, then, let's marry'? I wished I could see through to his true feelings, his real nature. Was this a trap or a test he was putting me to? Or was he convinced of my integrity and simply risking everything on one throw? I knew that a man would soon despise a woman who accepted such a proposal and took advantage of his weakness and his hysteria. For a moment his conscience might be suffocated by passion—but later?

He looked at me with his eyes full of tears. 'For me to be able to hurt so much a woman who will soon give birth to a child—a child of mine, Marevna—must I not truly love you?'

'Are you sure that it's not only that you believe you love me?

87

And after a while won't you be fed up with me because I've lent myself to this lie and shared with you in the betrayal of that woman?'

'You're so obstinate! Listen, and try to understand this. Angelina herself agrees that I should live with you. You and I, Marevna, do you understand? You'll come and live in my studio. She'll stay in the apartment with the child. And if you don't care for that arrangement, well, the two of us will go and live somewhere else. I'll leave you now. Think it over fully. I'll do whatever you want. But come and see Angelina one of these days, and she'll tell you herself she's willing to separate from me. She's kind and intelligent.'

He kissed my hand and went away.

I talked to myself in a kind of Dostoyevskyan monologue. 'Poor "kindly cannibal". I'm sorry for him—he's so weak. Yet, at the same time, I despise him for his cruelty towards a woman who is aging. When he met her she was twenty-five and he was barely twenty. I believe he had not much money then; she belonged to the best Tsarist society and was receiving an allowance from her father. At twenty-five she cannot have been ugly, in spite of her pointed nose and red cheeks. Even now she has kept her slimness and her passion for extraordinary hats, which she makes herself. She always reminds me of a little bird, a parakeet (and sometimes she screams with rage like a parakeet too). I cannot understand her letting her Diego Diegovich go without a struggle. But is she really letting him go? This intelligent woman, who looks so frail but possesses uncommon strength of mind, is doubtless staking everything on her baby. If it should be a boy Diego would not be able to desert it, for he would have an heir to bear his name and carry on his line. . . . How I would like to be strong too, and not throw myself with my eyes shut into a game in which my part will not be entirely to my advantage. . . . If I really loved Diego it would be better to put up with any affront and remain unmarried. Marriage is for Angelina, if she should ask it for the child's sake. If she wishes to have the best part and to act the victim in the eyes of the world, then I too will play fair and be kind, and not take advantage of the weakness and insensate passion of the "kindly cannibal" . . . Poor "kindly cannibal"—and poor little "sea princess".'

I went to talk the whole thing over with Ehrenburg, who told me I was an idiot. Life was short enough without deliberately adding complications. 'It will all work out, you'll see. The baby will be born, Angelina will stay, but you will have the right to all Diego's love. All that signifies is whether you love him or not.' In short, he urged me to throw myself into his friend's arms (not without a slightly sadistic curiosity about what would come of it all).

Diego came running to see me after having Angelina taken to a nuns' clinic for her lying-in. He asked me to go to his apartment and have a picnic lunch with him. We were not to talk about ourselves, he promised. 'In a day or two you shall go and see Angelina. She'll tell you everything, and after that we shall be free.'

The apartment was all upside down—socks with holes in them scattered everywhere and dirty underwear of Diego's that he did not quite manage to hide under the bed. There were some very fine pictures and I asked him whether one day he would give me one of his canvases as a present. A little canvas.

'Anything you want,' he said.

He was very gay as he prepared the *riz à la mexicaine*—quantities of rice and lots of olive oil, smelling of garlic, onions and pepper. I burst out laughing when I saw him screw up a corner of his handkerchief and tickle deep inside his nostrils, one after the other, sneezing violently each time.

'It clears my brain, which has been blocked for some time,' he explained.

The rice was splendid, and so were our appetites. We talked desultorily, in order not to be left with nothing to say. Then came the moment when Rivera led me towards a big armchair, sat down and put me on his knee. I had liked this very much in the past: like a good, trustful little girl I had sat on the knees of Gorki, Voloshin and Rivera himself. But now I had become someone else, and I was frightened—though heaven knows there was nothing immodest about us.

We stayed for a good time without moving. Then:

'Comfortable, Marevna?' he asked. He turned his face to me and I saw that his eyes were full of tears.

'Yes, quite. Extremely, in fact.'

What would I not have given if we could have had a bath before anything else? How could I tell this great child that in order to win a tigress's love, the tiger must be cleaner? I remembered Katya, when we were at Èze, giving Ehrenburg clean underclothes and shouting to him to brush his teeth ('Your breath stinks, Ilya!').

An idea came to me. 'I have a touch of rheumatism, Diego. I need to go to the hot baths. Will you come with me? We could go in together and you could have a bath too. It would be a way of washing off all the old dust. We'll be brand new.'

He agreed, and I asked him to put on clean linen and change his trousers too.

'I haven't any others,' he said.

'Then you must buy some. We'll see to that, and we can buy some shoes and underwear at the same time. I've seen the clothes drying in the kitchen—they're all in rags. It's not that it's very important, but it would be nice if you were a bit neater. You look like a tramp.'

He grumbled, protesting that he would need all his money to pay for Angelina's lying-in and that he was accustomed to doing without things.

'Oh, come,' I said. 'You're earning money. Don't you ever buy anything?'

'I give everything I earn to Angelina and she does what she likes with it. Look at my socks.' And he showed me his socks with holes in them, fastened to his torn underwear with safety pins.

I could not understand how Angelina could let her Diego Diegovich neglect himself to such a degree. Had she not declared to me that she cherished him like a child? But perhaps there was this about it too: the cherished child does not always lend itself so readily to the attentions of the mother.

The days passed and we savoured our freedom joyfully, like

devoted self-seekers. We made little purchases for Diego; we went to the Louvre; we walked along the embankments; we took a small boat down the Seine towards St Cloud. We were usually hand in hand, but I always went home to sleep. Then one evening, when we had been to the cinema, Diego insisted that I should spend the night at his apartment. I pointed out that this was hardly advisable, from his point of view and that of his concierge.

'We must live for our own sakes, not for the concierge,' he rejoined. 'Life is too short and we've wasted too much precious time already. When I think of all the months I've known you. . . . Come on. I won't hurt you.'

I went home with him and we sat by the fire without turning on any light. The moon gave plenty of illumination.

Suddenly he said, 'I want to see you naked by moonlight. I've never had the chance, as others have, of seeing you bathe in the sea. Do me this favour. I ask you in all humility.'

He besought me so gently that I could not refuse. He unfastened my clothes and I went to sit in an armchair, my naked body bathed in the moonlight. Rivera sat in an armchair opposite me, his hands and elbows resting on the arms. His eyes glowed in the half-light. 'A werewolf,' I thought.

At last I said I was sleepy. The moon was hypnotizing me. I wanted to go.

'Don't go,' he said. 'Stay. Don't be frightened. I'll be patient as long as you like, but stay.'

We slept in separate beds. I was considerate of Angelina, saying to myself, 'I am her guest here. She'll come back one day, and I don't want to leave a shadow of evil behind me.'

We lived like this for several days, getting used to each other's nakedness in all simplicity. We romped, running round the table, wrestling, rolling on a bed, pushing each other about, but I got away nimbly each time I saw the great, damp mouth open, as though the 'cannibal' were about to eat me up. I believe Rivera enjoyed these games too. I believe these were the best of all the moments that I spent living with him. Everything had been said, nothing consummated. We were children.

Angelina gave birth to a son, and Diego asked me to go to see her. My heart was beating rapidly as I went up to her room, but I was able to look her in the face. I had done nothing. Nothing had changed.

I found her in a darkened room, and in her bed she looked young again, pink and shining (all women shine like this when they have just given birth). In a cot by her bedside was a miniature Diego, red and wrinkled. I felt a pang, and almost wished the baby were mine. I loved him already. I hoped Angelina would let me help look after him.

'Good morning, Marevna,' she said, and at that moment Diego came in with a nun and two bouquets of flowers. One of the bouquets he placed on Angelina's bed and the other he gave to me, kissing my hand. He was so distraught that he did not even look at his son.

Angelina beckoned me to her side and murmured, with tears in her eyes, 'I know all about it, Marevna. Go with him if you love him. And be happy, both of you.' The tears streamed down her cheeks on to her white nightgown.

I felt foolish and ashamed, and for a moment I longed to be in her place, for wasn't it the better of the two? I had more compassion for her than ever before, and I should have liked to know whether Diego shared my feelings. He was pale and his features were twisted in the effort to smile, as they were whenever he was embarrassed or vexed. I wanted to tell him that it was all over, that I could not accept Angelina's sacrifice, but the words would not leave my throat. I kissed Angelina and fled, far away from that woman and 'her man', whom she was so generously presenting to me. I tossed away my lovely bouquet as I ran. I heard a call behind me—Rivera's voice—but I ran on.

I did not go back to my studio. I went to a café where I could hide, alone and undisturbed, for I knew that if I went home I should find Diego there. I believe that if I had had any money I would have gone away somewhere, anywhere. The café was near the Gare Montparnasse; it was full of travellers, tradesmen, commonplace old couples, young people, soldiers on leave in tête-à-tête with peroxided women. I stayed there till very late. At last I set off for my studio, slowly, looking in every direction in case the 'cannibal' was lying in wait for me. I saw no one.

But I had hardly opened my door when I felt his presence. He was lying on the sofa in the darkness, waiting for me.

'Where have you been? Why did you go away, Marevna? You've left me alone all day—I thought I was going mad.'

'Ah,' I thought, 'that's my great child. I love him, but as for depending on him to protect me and defend me from whatever might be. . . . What we ought to do is go away, far, far away. But alas, where can we go? There's the war, and we are poor.'

* * *

We became lovers.

When Angelina returned to the apartment Diego and I went to live in the studio. Our life became orderly. I worked with Diego in the studio or in the little room behind. Sometimes he ate with Angelina, sometimes with me. It was a hard winter. We were short of coal and I shivered in the enormous studio. One day Rivera came home with two presents for me. The first was a pair of little Siamese cats. They kept us warm at night, but soon they fell ill from the cold and, in spite of all my care, they died, one after the other. I was sorely grieved.

The second present made me blush hotly when I unwrapped it—a pink india-rubber hygienic device.

'It's a very prosaic present, *milaya*,' said Rivera.

Clearly he did not want any more children. But, rebelliously, I told myself that very day, 'I shall have one too, and it shall be more beautiful than the other. Otherwise, what's the use?' With Diego I had learned the keen joy of really being a woman; my maternal instinct had been roused along with my senses.

'Think of your painting and the splendid career that's waiting for you,' said Diego. 'You're madly gifted and you can be a good painter. There's nothing to stop you loving my child as if he were your own.'

93

But Angelina did not see things in the same way. It did not take me long to realize that she found my presence undesirable and that I must stop going up to the apartment to see the baby. I found many of Rivera's friends hostile to me, particularly Mme S., in whose house I no longer set foot. Diego sometimes accompanied Angelina there—'reluctantly', he told me.

'I can't do anything else, Marevna. She buys my pictures, and she'll buy yours too, to please me. An artist can't ignore these society women. Yes, they bore us stiff, of course, but they're useful. Almost indispensable.'

(Later on, Soutine was to tell me the same thing. I must admit I saw their point, but at the same time I despised them for their sycophancy.)

When Diego went off to the Ss' with Angelina, now recovered and becomingly dressed, I would feel sorry for myself, since all my frocks had worn out and I had practically nothing to wear.

'You're a thousand times more beautiful in a slip or nothing,' Diego would say, to pacify me (I have since come to believe that every man tells the same story to his wife or mistress, and that it is an excellent way of saving pennies.)

On those evenings and others when the baby was left alone, Marie Blanchard, an old friend of Diego's and Angelina's, came to look after him. She was a painter of mixed Polish, Spanish and French blood; among the women artists she was thought to be one of the most gifted. Her face was witchlike—bony, with a long nose and piercing eyes—and she had a hump on her back and in front. She did not like me, jealous because of her fondness for Rivera. He often told me with a laugh that it depended only on him whether he had a child by Marie—she was longing for it.

'Why not have it then? I'm sure she'd bring it up admirably.'

'I'm not so sure. It's myself she loves. She'd like to go to bed with me, if only once. But I feel quite incapable of it.'

Both Rivera and I did a lot of work, and he told me that it was a long time since he had felt such zeal and such ardour.

'You're the cause of it, you know. I'm happy. What about you?'

I answered that my happiness was so great that I quaked day

and night for fear of losing it, but I did not admit that I had a presentiment that I should pay dearly for these moments of happiness.

Crowds of people who were interested in modern painting came to the studio. André Lhote often came to 'talk painting' with Diego, who could talk for hours, drawing, explaining, turning pale and getting more and more agitated. Sometimes Matisse would drop in too, and Diego addressed the two by turns or both together, showing them his pictures and proving that each line, each angle, each cubic form was the result, not of pure chance, but extensive knowledge and careful study. I always listened eagerly, trying to understand so that I could use what I heard in my own work. Sometimes the impressive Diaghilev called to look at the work of Diego, who generously showed mine too. I saw Diego's growing importance among the artists, his energy, his intelligence and his goodness to his friends.

But his friendship could be changeable and uncertain. Sometimes he would speak of being 'sick of' so-and-so and disinclined to see him any more. His relations with Picasso, whom he admired exceedingly at times ('He's sensitive, cunning and skilful, and he's a genius at drawing. He wanted to be taken for a great painter, and he succeeded'), are a case in point. Picasso, invariably curious about other artists and anything they were doing that might be new and interesting, used to come to Rivera's studio and wander about freely, turning over canvases at will to look at them.

Rivera complained to me more than once. 'I'm sick of Pablo. If he pinches something from me, people will rave about Picasso, Picasso. As for me, they'll say I copy him. One of these days either I'll chuck him out or I'll shove off to Mexico.'

Soon afterwards, they nearly came to blows. 'He left when I picked up my Mexican stick and threatened to break his skull,' Rivera told me. I never learned the full details of this incident, but I know that for some time there was a coolness between the two painters.

Diego gave nearly all his money to Angelina and the child, and that left the two of us almost penniless. When we ate at the studio it was always very scantily. I obtained some money from the faithful Yura. I also earned money by painting portraits from photographs of great Jewish poets for a Russian *émigré* who had a printing press. I used the money to buy food and coal.

But the money I earned caused trouble. One evening, I came back late and Diego, looking grim, asked me where I had been. When I told him he became absolutely furious, and I thought he would strangle me. I realized that he was having one of his fits. He stammered incoherently, and all I could make out was that he was convinced I was deceiving him and that was where the money came from.

I got him to bed, and the next day he was in a high fever. Rosa, who cleaned for us, for Angelina and for a number of other painters, told Angelina that Diego was ill. In the evening an ambassadress from Angelina arrived—Mme S., all furs and scent. With scarcely a word to me, she sat down on the edge of Diego's bed and tried to persuade him to move to the apartment, where it was warmer. He said that I was looking after him perfectly and that it was quieter where he was.

I stood with my back to them, looking out of the window, feeling like an intruder. I knew that Diego was fighting for his liberty, but I was afraid of the effect the icy studio might have on him. At last I turned around and said, 'If Diego feels worse he shall move to the apartment. I'll have some coal tomorrow and it'll be warmer. You may be sure I'll do my best to make him well.'

'That's agreed, then,' Mme. S. said. '*Au revoir*. I'll tell Angela Mikhaylovna what you've promised.' She swept out regally.

Suddenly Diego began laughing—roaring with laughter.

'Go ahead and laugh,' I said. 'If you want to be looked after somewhere else, don't be shy. I'm not keeping you.'

'*Durochka*! *Detochka*! It's that woman who's making me laugh.'

'I can easily guess why. All these old hens who climb on poor artists' backs and get the name for being Maecenases—they're nothing but tarts. She was poor until she found herself a millionaire and got divorced to marry him. Now look at her!'

'Don't be angry, Marevna. I didn't ask her here.'

I nursed him as one can nurse someone who is more than dear. Though I had become used to his fits of 'lunacy', each time I was terrified for my own skin. A particularly violent attack coincided with his recovery. He suddenly began talking in a language entirely strange to me, seized me by the arm, knelt in front of an armchair and forced me to my knees at his side. He was livid and only the whites of his eyes were showing. Then, in the same strange language, he began to speak quickly, in an imploring tone, pausing at intervals as though awaiting a response. I remained motionless at his side, not daring to risk opposing him at such a moment.

At last he turned to me and said, in French, 'That's done. We are married before one of my Aztec ancestors. He consents that I should take you for my wife.'

'Who are you talking to now, Diego?' I asked, trembling.

'To Marevna,' he replied. Then, touching my face, my hair and my body: 'Yes, it's you, all right. Marevna.'

When he was having one of his fits, I could generally save myself by saying gently that I was Marevna and begging him not to hurt me. He would hesitate, sniff the air, and say, 'Yes, yes, I recognize your smell. I shan't hurt you.'

But it was not always like that, and I still bear on my neck a mark of his frenzy.

We were walking in Montparnasse and met Picasso, who casually touched my breasts and said how beautiful he thought they were. (This is a customary gesture of his. He did the same to my daughter in the summer of 1948, and I laughed when she angrily told me about it. Picasso will never change!) I stepped back, restraining an impulse to box his ears.

Diego went white and foamed with anger, but said nothing until we got home. Then he rounded on me. 'If Pablo touches your breasts so unceremoniously it must mean that you're sleeping with him. Come on, confess!'

I only laughed.

'I knew it already,' he went on. 'I saw a sketch of a nude at his place and recognized at once that it was a drawing of you.'

'Lots of women look alike in nude sketches. Did you ask him who it was?'

'No. He wouldn't have told the truth. But I know what you look like so well that I didn't have to ask!'

Now I was angry too. 'I've never been at his house alone—to my great regret.'

The words drove him to fury. With one hand he twisted my arms behind my back; with the other he seized a *navaja* (clasp-knife) that was lying on the table, opened it, and placed the point against my throat. I begged him in a faint voice to have pity on his loving, faithful Marevna. He was trembling as much as I was. I felt the knife prick my throat. I fainted.

When I came to, I was lying on the floor, with the open knife inches away. Rivera was gone. My neck was stinging. I got up and staggered over to the looking glass: I was covered with blood.

I washed myself and made a dressing with a towel and a hand-kerchief. Then, aching all over, feeling my legs buckling under me, I lay down on the bed and thought about Diego. Where was he? Was he trying to frighten me into leaving him? Was he sorry? What was I to do? It was a nightmare. I resolved that no one would know; I would clean the knife and hide it in the coal scuttle.

Later Diego came back, full of remorse. 'I didn't know what I was doing, Marevna. I'm mad. Mad with jealousy of all the men who knew you before me. Tell me you never slept with Pablo. Tell me truly that Ilya has never been your lover. Swear!'

I swore, knowing that he did not believe me, and he swore not to belong to Angelina. The jealousies of men and women! I was as guilty as he. I was jealous of other women. I was particularly jealous of Mme S., to whom Diego had given an engraving he had promised to me. On that occasion she had made some excuse to pull up her skirt nonchalantly and let Diego have a good look at an expanse of white thigh. I saw his eyes shine. We quarrelled after she had gone, and he laughed at my jealousy, as he always did. Scenes like this usually culminated in a fight, which he won. He would patiently, slowly tie my hands and feet as I lay on the bed or the floor, relishing his own strength, my defeat, my weakness and my amorous surrender.

Rivera sometimes told me that Angelina disliked our living so near her. I said I was prepared to return to my studio in the rue Asseline, but he said no, I should certainly fall ill there with no coal and no one to look after me. I saw that he was torn between his love for me and his duty to Angelina and the baby, and I felt pity for his weakness of character. Perhaps if he had had the money to support two households things would have been different. The means he chose to resolve his dilemma was cowardly. He told me that Mme S. wanted to see me. I went, and was told that my presence in Diego's studio was torture to Angelina because she could hear us from the apartment; I was offered money to move. I responded with bravado, refusing the money grandly and boasting that it would take more than moving to separate Diego from me, but the meeting left me trembling, burning with shame for this woman and the game she was voluntarily playing between Diego and me. When I got home, Diego was waiting for me, and I could see at a glance that he had known the purpose of the meeting before sending me. I was disgusted at his weakness, and terrified at the same time.

I left, with my box of paints under one arm and the basin in which I used to wash the 'kindly cannibal' under the other. At the rue Asseline I found a money order from Yura. Hardly had I set foot inside the door when Diego arrived, begging me to come to the post office with him. There was, he said, some money for him there, and we could rent a room somewhere in Montparnasse. When I discovered the money was a money order from Mme S. for five hundred francs, I was furious. I told him to keep his money for himself. I had received some of my own—much, much cleaner—from Russia. I accused Mme S. of trying to get rid of me so that she could come and see him at his studio without embarrassment.

'How absurd you are!' he answered.

We were still arguing as we started in search of a room to give shelter to our unsettled love and serve as a studio for me. We found one at last, centrally heated, comfortable and pleasant to work in, with a lavatory and two big windows looking out along the boulevards Montparnasse and Raspail (of course one could see the Rotonde and the Dôme). Rivera insisted on paying the first month's rent. I let him because I was terrified of falling ill when I was penniless, and I moved in for the winter.

Diego started a big cubist portrait of me, *décolletée*, showing a lot of leg in transparent stockings and stitting in an armchair. The armchair was quite near the window and I could feel a draft on my back, but I said nothing about this. The picture promised well and I enjoyed watching him work. From time to time, however, I felt a twinge in my left side and thought I should be lucky if I did not get pneumonia.

Then for two days Diego did not come. Early the third morning, I suddenly felt very ill. I needed poulticing and cupping. How could I let him know? Painfully I dressed and set out for the rue du Départ. It was pure madness! Angelina came to the door and kept me standing on the cold stairway; she would not have let me see Diego if he had not heard us talking and come to the door too.

'I'm ill and alone, Diego,' I said. 'Why haven't you come to see me? Aren't you allowed out any more?'

Angelina stood watching us in silence.

'I'll come at once,' he promised. 'Run off quickly, Marevna. I've been ill too.'

I ran down the stairs like a madwoman, choking with shame, furious with myself for coming where I was hated, loathed. I knew that Diego would be furious too. It was cold out of doors but I was covered with sweat when I got back to my room. I could hardly breathe. I threw myself on the bed, sure I was in for an attack of pleurisy.

Diego arrived raging, but seeing how ill I was mollified him, and he merely asked me why I had come to upset Angelina.

I retorted that he should have come as he had promised and that I had not enjoyed having to go and hunt him up. 'And now please go to the chemist's and bring something to rub me with and something to make poultices. I don't want to die here to gratify your wife.'

He came back with what looked like the entire contents of a chemist's shop and, when I had been daubed with medicine and wrapped in cotton-wool, he sat on the edge of the bed and fondled me.

'You're devilish,' he said. 'A real little savage. But I love you like that. Listen, I'll have a hot drink brought up, and then I'll go and find Dagusya. She'll come and keep you company. I'll come later and see how you're getting on.'

He kissed me and left me alone.

Dagusya was a friend of both of us, a delightful girl from Tiflis, a painter and a dedicated one, but possessed of a talent that was only average. She had a heart of gold and everyone adored her. Many times she had said to me, with a laugh, 'You're mad to be smitten with Rivera, a beautiful girl like you! There are plenty of men about you who are handsomer, quite ready to shower attentions on you and let you live in clover. What do you see in the great gorilla?'

I answered that it was true he looked like a gorilla, but it was like Beauty and the Beast: the better one knew him the handsomer one thought him.

'You're quite crazy,' she said, 'but so long as your fairy tale makes you happy. . . . If only it lasts!'

'It will last as long as I want it to,' I said, challenging the gods.

Gradually Dagusya began to discover that Diego could be charming, when he wanted to be, and that one could forget his great belly and his flat feet. He understood women, loved them all, I honestly believe, and had an instinctive sense of what to say that would please them most.

Diego and Dagusya nursed me. Each day Dagusya brought food, and warmed it up on a spirit stove and we had little dinners à trois. After a few days I was over the worst, but I still could not sit for my portrait. Diego, with his artist's selfishness, did not conceal his vexation at the length of my illness.

It was a very good portrait, although he was merciless in his depiction of me. A white, triangular wash took the place of the face; one could guess it to be me from the fair hair. The simplicity of it was magnificent. When it was finished I asked Rivera to give it to me, but he took it jealously away.

* * *

With the first suns of spring I came back to the rue Asseline. I furnished my studio more pleasantly, buying a new bed and mattress and getting hold of a special lamp in order to see better in the evenings. But certain things I could do nothing about. The lavatories were in the yard, and it was hardly pleasant to have to get up in the middle of the night, find one's way down the stairs in the dark and expose oneself half naked to the night chill. I was always afraid that Diego, who refused to use the bucket, would fall down the stair well. At last he settled for the window.

While I was ill I had written to Yura and to Max Voloshin. Yura had answered that I must come to Moscow as quickly as possible and Gorki would introduce me to the physician Mechnikov, who would very soon get me well. Max had written that if I continued to be ill and unhappy, he and his mother would expect me at Yalta, where there was the sun and everything necessary to restore me and raise my spirits. I showed Diego these letters and told him he must not imagine that if I stayed in Paris it was because my prospects had been checked or because I was abandoned by my friends. No, if I stayed in Paris it was solely for his sake, because I loved him and him alone. I hoped he would be able to understand, to judge my decision at its true value and form a precise estimate of the utter, disinterested gift of myself that I was making.

Little by little I was beginning to understand Rivera through and through, but my youthfulness, my high spirits, my love prevented my having with him the necessary patience and composure. Moreover (unhappily for me) I burned with passion for him. One day, after we had been quarrelling (I do not remember why) and had finally made it up, he came over to kiss me. I held up my lips, drew him towards me with one hand and with the other stabbed

102

him with a knife in the back of the neck. I was so mad with jealousy that I wanted to hurt him as he had hurt me.

He burst into loud laughter and, as he staunched the blood that was dripping over his shirt, said almost gaily, 'You flatter me, Marevna.'

'You flattered me too,' I answered, showing him my own neck and the disfiguring scar. 'I shall certainly carry this mark till I die.'

As he carried his: before he left for Mexico I saw a slight white scar on his neck, just below the hairline.

During the whole of our liaison, from 1915 to 1921, I was faithful to him, body and soul. Of course, I was often slandered by those who were trying to detach him from me. Sadly, because most of the women he had known were flighty, he tended to credit the slanders. If he happened to find a man sitting for his portrait in my studio he would rush away, and if I followed him out to the landing he would hurl a curse at me and not come back for a day or two. He wanted me to work only at my own painting, but he never gave me the money that would have allowed me to do this; so I had to earn some, and one of the simplest ways was to find friends who commissioned portraits. But Rivera accepted my explanations with great reluctance and refused to believe that I could remain faithful in the midst of the many men who were making up to me.

And yet, in spite of all these tempests, our happiness was greater than at any other time during the first two years. I dashed about like a mad thing to earn a little money, so I could give him a dinner he would like. After dinner we often drew, both sitting at the table. He showed me the copies he had made of Cézanne, El Greco, Giotto and the Flemish painters, talking eloquently about his work, his pictures, his ambitions. Sometimes he would let himself go, becoming very gay, almost boyish. With a glass of wine on his head he would shake his great hips and his huge belly in a parody of a Mexican dance, and I would laugh till I cried. He would sing too, with his eyes sparkling and his mouth wearing a broad, happy smile.

He used to talk about Mexico, one minute with passionate

intensity, the next with amusement. (Ilya Ehrenburg once observed that Diego always went from one extreme to the other: he could never live or feel like everyone else.)

'I was born at Guanajuato,' he told me. 'My grandfather was born in Spain and bore the title of marquis. I'm telling you the truth, *ditya*—I can show you the papers. He was an extraordinary man, you know. He didn't get married till he was fifty, and then to a beautiful Mexican girl of Portuguese descent who was only seventeen, Ynés Acosta. At sixty-two he joined Benito Juarez in the War of Reform and then enlisted in the Mexican army against the French.

'My father, Don Rivera, whom I'm very fond of, as you know, is a man of great courage. He married Maria del Pilar Barrientos. Her father was a telegraph operator in a Spanish mine. He was more than liberal in his views. Her mother was half Spanish, half Indian. I was very fond of her too.

'In 1886 Maria was brought to bed of twins, myself and a brother born a few minutes later. I was so weakly that in order not to frighten my mother the midwife ordered a servant to put me away somewhere. I was put in a dung bucket. It was my grand-mother who found me and nursed me back to life. She did what Indian women do—she killed some pigeons and wrapped their warm intestines round me, rubbed me with medicinal herbs and thumped me, calling softly, "Venga, venga, muchachito. Venga, nino!" and I came back to life, to my grandmother's great renown.

'I was very mechanically minded. I told my father and mother that I wanted to be an engineer, a doctor and a painter—all of them! My father congratulated me and encouraged me, but my mother cherished an ambition to see me a soldier. . . . When I was ten, I was sent to the San Carlos Fine Arts Academy. Later on I went and studied at Madrid, Toledo and Barcelona. When I came to Paris for the first time, and had my first sight of pictures by Cézanne and Rousseau, I was knocked flat. I liked Picasso very much too, but I was still under the influence of Toloiga—I worked at his studio. I went everywhere. Italy, Belgium, Holland, England.

'I went back to Mexico for a time, and then a revolution started.

You know the Mexican temperament. It's like a volcano, continually working underground. It boils up and suddenly bursts and begins to spit fire and vomit lava. In 1914 I returned to Spain and afterwards to Paris.'

'I told him I had seen him for the first time in Rosalie's *crémerie*, looking just like a Moor, wearing a workman's blue overalls and all smeared with paint, especially on the behind, because that is where one wipes one's fingers and brushes. I had liked him at once; I had liked his head.

'*Ditya*, you were an adorable girl. Madame S. used to laugh at you and call you the *gimnazistka* (high school girl), but I thought you were charming—unspoiled, enthusiastic, volatile. That is why I fell in love with you. And we wasted a year before we went to bed together! You fled from me as though I were a policeman!'

Listening to Diego's talk, I found it all fascinating. Whatever he might have been, he was no boring mediocrity. Genius emanated from his pores. Is it any wonder women forgot his ugliness and came to love him?

I saw to it that he was clean. I washed his feet, which were very sensitive. He let his behind and his head be washed like a small child. It is a fact that he did not like water. It was really funny to watch him begin to wash himself in the morning. He would stand a long time in front of the basin of soapy water before he made up his mind to wash his face, motionless, gazing at some point in space (perhaps at these moments he saw lines and colours arranging themselves). Sometimes I lost patience, jumped out of bed and plunged his head into the basin. Then he would make all sorts of animal noises with his mouth and nostrils. After the ablutions came the rite of cleaning out his nose with a corner of a handkerchief, which I always found hilarious.

* * *

Rivera became very fond of some new friends, the Fishers, who were Danes. The man was a gifted sculptor, well-known in his own country, and his wife painted. They lived at Arcueil, where Diego often went to see them. I was most anxious to make their acquaintance and a little hurt at not being able to do so. But, since our affair had begun, I was as though enclosed in a magic circle, unable to meet any of Diego's friends—not those, at all events, whom Angelina saw. As for my many friends, I did not care to see them now, for fear of being slandered or coming under one influence or another. I preferred to be alone. I lived wrapped up in myself, my work and my love. I would usually stay at home waiting for Diego, or he would arrange to meet me somewhere and we would stroll along the boulevards in the warm night fragrant with chestnut blossoms. Sometimes we would lie down on the still young grass of the fortifications, or sit in the darkness of a secluded seat, and lose ourselves in the depths of loving tenderness. I was so much shorter than Rivera that in order to put my arms round his neck I had to stand on tiptoe, and I literally hung from his lips. He laughed as he supported me like this, pleased at his own strength. Or he would cradle me in his arms like a child. At such moments I forgot my resentment, having to play second fiddle, my loneliness, my poverty. I was young, sanguine and I believed in a great love. What was the paltriness of life beside all that?

Frequently Diego showed me his drawings and asked me whether I liked them. He tried several times to make pencil portraits of me, and some of them were successful (they were stolen from me later). I very much liked his manner of drawing: the delicacy of line reminded me of Ingres; the construction was firm and sure. Later on his drawing assumed greater sharpness—clean lines with no retouching—and the portraits he made of all kinds of people were remarkable for their characterization and accuracy. He was already preparing for his great frescoes, in each of which his touch is at once recognizable—spacious, simple, clean, strong, and profoundly true.

He gave a small exhibition of drawings. I went by myself, and was delighted with what I saw. The drawings were priced at two hundred and fifty francs each. I knew he was in need of money (what artist is not?) and I bought one (unfortunately, all I could afford). I took it home and hung it on the wall. When Diego came to see me, I asked him whether he was pleased with the sales at his exhibition, and he answered that not a day passed but a drawing was sold and that if all went well he would be able to give me a little money.

When he was in bed he suddenly caught sight of the drawing hanging at the other end of the studio. He jumped out of bed, stark naked, and ran to make sure his eyes were not playing tricks on him.

'Who bought you that, Marevna? It's the best one I showed.'

I answered that I had made myself a present of it. He was furious. Come to his show and buy one of his works? Me? It was madness! I told him I had done it with all my heart, in gratitude for the help he had given me at times.

'No, no, *ditya*! It's impossible. You must have your money back. And I'll bring you some more drawings as well. You must have them to please me.'

I need hardly say that I was enchanted.

Whenever he spent the night with me, I used to go in the morning for hot *croissants*, milk and newspapers. We played at being married, and I enjoyed it very much, probably because it did not happen every day. Then he would go home to start work, and I would start too.

'Work! You must work!' he used to say. 'If only Angelina and Marie were not so inefficient! I'd arrange a fine exhibition for you. But what's the use? They make me sick!'

He regularly blamed someone else for whatever did not go right in his house or in his work. There came a day when Angelina, wishing to be free to devote herself more completely to Diego and his work, placed little Diego in a children's home in Chaville. They used to go to see him together every Sunday.

It was bitter grief to me not to be in a position where I could see the child again, and I said as much to Diego.

'Don't worry, you'll see him all right one day,' he said, to pacify me.

107

Soon afterwards he confided to me that the child was not well and that they had decided to bring him home again. Then Diego began to complain that Angelina did not know how to look after the child properly. She was consulting a book by a German doctor, but it did not help because all the women she knew—and all their friends—interfered with advice. Diego raged against 'all these kind women'. I reproached him for being so feeble and told him the child would be better tended in a hospital than at home, where all three slept in one small room. He said he was sickened by interference from all sides and was letting Angelina do as she pleased. I saw very well that he was unhappy, and I was unhappy for him. He could no longer work peacefully, being preoccupied with the health of the child, who was now a year and a half old, but 'very big for his age and quite exceptional,' Rivera said. I hoped with all my heart that little Diego would get better, to rejoice his father and (in my secret soul) myself.

The winter came. A particularly cold winter, terrible months for me and for everyone in the poor part of Paris. There was no water in my studio in the rue Asseline, and I had to go down to the yard with my jug and bucket to draw it—provided the tap was not frozen. Often I had to wash my face at the café. I could not manage to keep warm, though I burned chairs, window-sashes, even picture frames. My hands were chapped and it hurt me to hold my brushes and palette. Short of warm clothes, I asked Diego to make me a present of his old overcoat (he now had a good Raglan coat which we had bought together in the rue St André-des-Arts), but he told me that the old coat was being used to stuff up the window in the bedroom, to prevent a draught on the child.

The seemingly endless war continued. When an air-raid alarm sounded, one was supposed to jump out of bed and dash out into the street and into a shelter—the depths of dismalness. Because of the alarms Rivera came seldom to make love to me. He and Angelina used to take shelter in the cellar of their house or in a Métro station. I myself, for the most part, walked about the streets, a prey to terror and distress. Or I slipped into the *crémerie* where I had been a regular customer and where I still sometimes ate, on credit. One could crawl in through an opening low down on the iron shutter, and once inside one was enveloped in pleasant warmth. I drank chocolate, tea or a glass of wine if I was treated to it by a kind friend (there was generally one there), and we would stay talking nonsense till the alarm was over. There were even people who contrived to get drunk, and following the all clear one saw them coming out of the *crémerie* on unsteady legs, describing comic arabesques on the boulevard.

If Diego happened to be with me at the rue Asseline when there was an alarm, we would put out the lamp and go to bed. My conscience would prick me and I would suggest that he return to the rue du Départ for Angelina's sake. But he would assure me that she and the baby were safe in the cellar and promise to go later. Though I cannot say that I was particularly proud of myself—or of him—at these times, I was overjoyed to have him near me. Lying side by side in the warmth of the bed, we forgot the alarm and all the fuss of everyday life, and lived our life *à deux*. After love comes tenderness and companionship.

'It hurts me to know that you've had other lovers,' he would tell me gently. 'I sometimes think of killing you, and I have a desire to mark you for life, so that you will never forget me.'

He had a bee in his bonnet about Ehrenburg. Had Ilya been my lover or not? And Voloshin? And Savinkov? And Gorki? He wanted to know the names of other Russian friends. I told him candidly that all that belonged to the past, and that I wanted to know nothing from him about anybody.

'Yes, because you don't really give a rap about me,' he said with a laugh.

He told me that Apollinaire had been responsible for Marie Laurencin's success, and added, 'That's what you need, a friend like that. I myself haven't got enough influence or authority here to help you as you ought to be helped.' I said it didn't matter, that everything would come to me if I might go on working at his side. When I gave up Cubism for Pointillism, I was beset with memories of the Caucasus, by visions of its mosaics, tapestries and frescoes. Contrary to the advice of Rivera, who told me not to spend too long on Surat's form of Impressionism (though he also told me my work was good and unlike anyone else's), I kept to the same manner for many years. Often I was discontented and discouraged because I could do neither more nor better work, but by persistence I managed to endow my subjects with transparence, volume, relief and a proper sense of proportion in their composition. Once Signac wrote me a letter of introduction to Felix Fénéon, and it said, among other things, 'I believe that if it had been possible for Seurat to see the water-colours and certain oil paintings by Marevna he would have been charmed by the freshness and vigour of her art,' and Fénéon too liked what I was doing. I have always believed that neither period nor fashion counts for anything if the work is beautiful.

Diego wanted me to work, but when I begged him to bring me materials I had run short of, he delayed, he forgot, or was himself without what I needed. When I managed to get myself a good brush or a fine new palette, he would beg me to lend it to him ('I shall think of you when I'm using it'). And I had not the courage to reproach him for his selfishness and lack of feeling.

Essentially, he resented my living the same life as before—out of jealousy, perhaps, because there had always been too many men around me. 'There are really three people in you, Marevna,' he said to me once. 'One boy—you're very like one of my comrades, who is dead—and two women, one who is simple and well behaved, almost angelic as Ilya says, and another who is just the opposite. It's this other that everyone likes and that attracts men. Frankly, why aren't you a courtesan? It would suit your capabilities perfectly.'

To which I replied, half vexed, half sorrowful, 'I know quite well that then I should have everything I lack. And so would you. But I know also that I should not have the unadorned happiness that I want. I should belong to everyone and no one. I should not be able to love a poor man because there would always be a rich man to pester me. There's only one thing about it that I should like—being able to help the artists around me, the girl-mothers

and their children. And you, do you think you would love me
more?'

'Very hard to answer. But I believe I couldn't share the woman
I love with everyone, or even with one other. Impossible. What is
possible is that I should desire you the more because of that. . . .
But touch a woman who shared her bed with someone else? No,
never!'

As I listened I told myself that perhaps this was not entirely
true—not the rock bottom of his thoughts.

When he did not come to see me I used to run round and wait
outside his house, whistling a tune he knew well. He would hurry
to the lavatory window and throw me a newspaper, with a few
words scrawled on it in charcoal to tell me whether he was coming
or not. But then the child fell ill, and after that I used to wait by
the Edgar-Quinet Métro station, where I had a view of Diego's
windows; if there was a white towel in the lavatory window it
meant that he was coming. Sometimes Angelina took the towel
away.

Time passed and little Diego did not get better. Rivera sometimes looked in in haste to give me news of him. One evening he
came in very pale, looking utterly wretched. Without taking off
his coat he said that he must go back at once, that the child was
worse and his life feared for. I did not know what to say. All words
are ineffectual in the face of great misfortunes.

'If only there weren't the war! The everlasting war! Could we
have done better for the child? Left him at Chaville? You'd
catch your death from the damp there. Brought him home?
There's no comfort, and we're always short of coal.'

But also, he might have said, he and Angelina would sometimes
go out and leave the child alone, and he would work the bedclothes
off. There was more than the war to blame. Perhaps an artist's
child is sacrificed too often to the selfishness of its parents. A child
upsets one's way of living, requires attentions that are not always
given, either out of negligence or thoughtlessness. (I was to learn
later, from friends, that Angelina accused me of being the real
cause of her little one's death. I wonder to this day how that could

have been possible, but doubtless a scapegoat was required. She could not have hurt me more deeply.)

Several days passed. I haunted the Métro station, keeping watch on Diego's windows. I sensed what was happening behind them, and I shared the pain of the household. Then one evening, when I was lying on my bed in the dark, I heard Rivera's slow, heavy tread on the stairs. I felt my heart turn over. I knew. Even before he came in and, as usual, stopped to hang his hat and stick on the screen, I knew. He came to the bed and sank down almost on top of me.

'It's over,' he said.

Simple words, but heavy with the fullness of his grief and despair at having seen the child he adored suffer and die. We remained silent a long time. I stroked his head gently and dried his tears, and at last he fell into a fatigued sleep by my side.

When he woke up he said, 'I must go back. I can't leave Angelina in this state. She's miserable. But the apartment weighs me down—it's painful to me now. I've been told I ought not to have children, Marevna, because they wouldn't live. Don't tell yourself any more that I might have a child by you—it would be a disaster.'

I said that if the child came from me things would be different, because I was much younger than Angelina and in robust health; that if I had a baby I shouldn't sacrifice it for anyone and should do everything to spare it sickness and poverty. 'Diego, perhaps it's not the right moment to say all this to you, but I know that Mexicans do not look on death as Europeans do. Your son has gone away, but he will come back one day in another body. Believe me! And, if one day I give you a daughter, promise me to love her.'

He could not repress a laugh, feeble and hollow. 'She'll have no luck, like all girls—like you, *ditya*.'

Little Diego was buried the next day. Standing behind a tree in the avenue du Maine, I watched the hearse and several carriages go slowly by. I followed the *cortège* on foot to the Montrouge cemetery. The cold was cruel and biting, but the sun shone to give me courage. At the cemetery I saw them all get out of the carriages. Diego was supporting Angelina, who was swathed in veils. I could not help thinking they both looked faintly ridiculous: he, tall and broad and more enormous than ever in his Raglan overcoat; she, small and slim, her tiny feet perched on high heels (she had very pretty shoes, I remember). Once again I followed, slipping from tree to tree, to the open grave. My eyes were burning with the cold and with tears. I shut them. When I opened them again everyone was leaving. I let them go and went up to the grave with a few flowers I had brought. The gravedigger had started shovelling in earth, working quickly to keep warm. I stood gazing at the rapidly filling hole that would keep the little body forever—the body which had promised so much. I left my flowers with the others beside the little cross inscribed 'Diego Rivera' and left, promising myself I would come back.

I had to go home on foot. I hardly felt the ground under me, for my legs seemed to be made of wood. When I reached the rue Asseline I was frozen, and I wept, out of grief and out of vexation because I could not make the stove catch. My fingers refused to obey me—and yet, God knows, I would willingly have given all ten fingers, if that could have brought the child back.

* * *

October 1917 saw the revolution in Russia so long awaited by the emigrants. When the amnesty came, many of them made preparations to return to their homeland. At the Rotonde and Delevsky's canteen, people would greet each other with a holiday cheerfulness, asking 'Are you going? When? Alone or with your family?' just as if they were at a railway station. My Russian friends began to vanish. Ehrenburg went off with Katya and Tikhon, and so did Lunacharsky, Aleksinsky, Markov and many of the habitués of the Rotonde. Max Voloshin was already in Russia. Everyone who went back anticipated better conditions for creative work and better earnings, counting on employment in theatre décor and professorships in new schools. Some, like David

Schoenberg and Marc Chagall, actually became Commissars of Art in Soviet Russia, and Chagall was even made Minister of Art at one time. (When Schoenberg came to Paris in 1921 to arrange the Soviet pavilion at the international exhibition, he gave me work decorating the pavilion and allowed me to exhibit my tapestries for furniture and fashions in a window at the Grand Palais.)

I was urged to go too. But there was Rivera to keep me. Moreover, I hardly knew my relatives and, although I had friends, I could not expect that I, who had taken no part in building the revolution and was living only for myself and for art, should be given a high position among the young Russian artists. I would have to begin my struggle all over again, whereas in Paris my work was beginning to be appreciated and written about.

I was not the only one to refuse repatriation. Many Russian artists preferred to stay in Paris, where they thought they were safe from danger. Soutine was unwilling to return to the place from which he had escaped with such difficulty; in addition, he feared that his work, too, would be misunderstood and rejected as it had been during his early years in Paris. Those of us who remained behind—Zadkine, Archipenko, Orlova and Vassilieva, to name a few—were nevertheless very interested in events in Russia and in the new culture.

Europe was deeply disturbed by the Russian revolution. Leaders of state saw 'Bolshevik ideas' as a great danger to themselves, and their fear of 'contamination' was reflected in the view and opinions of the bourgeois press. Anything that shocked, belittled or antagonized the bourgeoisie came to be described as 'the Bolshevik threat'. Inevitably, Cubism, which stood for freedom and against the retrograde tastes of the bourgeoisie, fell into this category. Soon the terms 'Bolshevism' and 'Cubism' were virtually synonymous in the public mind. Charlatans, swindlers, madmen, socialists (who did not conceal their political views and openly spoke their minds), artists—all these were lumped together and pigeonholed with a contemptuous, 'Well, of course he's a cubist, a Bolshevik. What can you expect?'

For the Russian colony, life in Paris became more difficult still when the Bolsheviks signed a separate peace with Germany. Concierges whose husbands, lovers, sons and brothers were fighting at the front began to persecute their Russian lodgers. 'Those dirty Russians,' one heard everywhere. 'Traitors! Spies! All the Russians in Paris ought to be sent packing! And given a kick in the behind too!'

Virulent anti-Russian feeling involved me in a most unpleasant incident. One morning, as I came out of my studio with my portfolio under my arm, my path crossed that of a market girl from Les Halles. In her black stockings and sabots, her short, pleated skirt and low-necked blouse, she made a splendid picture as she pushed her barrow of fruits and vegetables along, humming to herself. Anyone would have stopped to admire, and I did.

'Well, what are you staring at?' she growled. 'It's a bit thick! What've I got that's so funny? Don't know, eh? Well, I'll tell you what I've got! I've got a brother at the war, and I work, I do, you whore! Codfish! I bet you're a foreigner!'

I did not deny it.

'What country are you from?'

I could have said Italy or America, but I did not care to lie.

'I knew it! Another one of those dirty Russians eating our children's bread!'

Releasing her barrow, she ran up to me and began shouting in my face. My silence seemed to provoke her more than anything I might have said. I tried to push her aside and escape, but she seized me by the shoulders, wrenched at my cape and snatched off my hat. I thought she was going to tear me to pieces.

She tried to incite the crowd that was collecting against me. 'We know the Russians now! Trash! Funks! Traitors! What are we waiting for? Why don't we take all of them who are still in Paris and break their backs?'

Whereupon she gave me furious clouts on both cheeks. My head struck the wall behind me and I lost consciousness momentarily.

The next thing I knew, a policeman was holding me by the arm. 'Don't take it to heart, mademoiselle. She is drunk. I know her well.' He let me go and went over to the the barrow girl, who was still shouting. 'Shut up, you! It would be a fine thing, if all the women were like you and talked like that. Off with you!'

Several of the onlookers expressed their sympathy for me, and I stopped at a *crémerie* to have a good cry. My face was burning and my lip was split.

One morning Diego and I were startled out of sleep by an explosion. For a moment I thought that a bomb had fallen on the house (I confess that there were times when I almost wished one would). Trembling, we pulled on our clothes and rushed out into the street. There were huge holes in a neighbouring street, the fronts of several houses and a small bar had been destroyed, a pregnant woman had been killed—Big Bertha having some fun. All day long she sowed panic among the population, and at night it was the aeroplanes. At the front, more and more friends were killed or wounded. Increasingly, one gave in to one's dread in spite of oneself, and worked badly.

In the chaotic atmosphere of tormented bodies, minds were continually overstimulated by alcohol and drugs. Several years earlier, I had experimented with hashish, which was then becoming the rage in Montparnasse. We ate the paste in little pellets or mixed it with tobacco and smoked it. The effect on me was usually a desire to laugh, followed by a fit of weeping or chattering about everything I saw (or thought I saw). At first I liked the drug because of the extreme, almost frightening lucidity I gained from it. Then one day I jumped through a window to the roof of the next house, imagining it was just below (it wasn't). I escaped with only a sore behind, and the roof with some broken slates, but that cooled my enthusiasm for hashish and for drugs in general. However, now and again I yielded to curiosity, to a desire to see great men behaving like madmen, or like hysterical school children. I must say that I was present at only a few bacchanals, and each time I had the sensation of being alien to my surroundings, each time I brought away an aftertaste of bitter despair, for the despondency of the participants was contagious.

Vivid in my memory, and fairly typical of those war-torn years, was an evening with Modigliani and Max Jacob in Montmartre. At the time Modi was living with the second of the three important women in his life, the Englishwoman, Beatrice Hastings, intelligent and a devotee of the arts, but dissipated, with strong tastes for alcohol, drugs and men. Their life together was tempestuous and marked by violent rows, such as the one at the Rotonde after he had locked her out of her apartment, which culminated in his receiving a sound thrashing and becoming *persona non grata* at the Rotonde (thereafter he went to the Dôme).

To reach the party we went up steps from the street, through a little garden and into a well-lighted room on the ground floor, furnished with a bureau, a table, chairs, a sofa, shelves full of books, a mountain of sandwiches and bottles of every kind. The guests that evening were Ehrenburg and Katya, Vitya Rosenblum, a Russian engineer and mathematician, Paul Cornet, André Delhay, Mitrani, a Greek philosopher, Carmen, a girl from Montparnasse, and me. For a while things were tame enough: Mitrani and Carmen, both somewhat drunk, making love on the sofa; Max Jacob and Delhay standing near the bureau discussing poetry and philosophy and watching the sofa; Ehrenburg, Katya and myself singing Russian songs (or rather shouting them, for none of us had much in the way of a voice).

Modigliani and Beatrice Hastings, far gone in drink, began one of their arguments. It quickly turned into a fight, with the two of them pommelling and kicking each other. The next thing we knew, he had seized her and hurled her through the closed window. A shattering of glass, a scream, and all that remained visible of Beatrice Hastings was her legs, dangling over the window sill—the rest of her was in the garden.

Everyone rushed from the room to go to her assistance. I took a wrong turning, opened a door, and found myself in a room where Vitya Rosenblum was on his knees, making the sign of the cross over and over again. Of Jewish descent and a Catholic convert like Max Jacob, Vitya was a virgin and religious to the point of bigotry.

'O God, save us from the accursed one and preserve us from

Diego, Modi, Ehrenburg

sin,' Vitya intoned in Russian, and touched the floor with his forehead.

I went out without a word, somewhat comforted by the knowledge that someone was looking after us.

Beatrice Hastings was carried in and laid on the sofa. Her long, flat breasts were daubed with blood; she was sober now, and utterly wretched. She wept, while Modigliani repeated, '*Non mea culpa, non mea culpa*'. The Greek, excited by the shouts and the tears and blood, pulled Carmen out into the garden, where we heard them staggering on the broken glass. The party resumed. Beatrice Hastings was given some coffee and wrapped up in a Scotch plaid, and Modi began telling her jokes to distract her.

At dawn we abandoned a battlefield. The room was littered with strips of paper torn from the walls, bottles and broken glasses, plates, food, overturned furniture. On the floor, motionless as corpses, were the bodies of the sleepers: Mitrani with Carmen clasped in his arms; Beatrice Hastings with her head under a sofa cushion; Max Jacob with a missal in his hand. Modigliani was still on his feet, methodically tearing the remains of the wallpaper off the walls and singing '*Capelli biondi vestita bianca*'.

The war came to an end at last. There was a frenzied celebration of the Armistice, a witches' sabbath in the streets of Paris; one could hardly push through the crowds of people, many with bottles in their hands, whirling and dancing (as in one of Soutine's pictures), embracing and kissing each other. Life had triumphed over death, and the future seemed to promise something for everyone. So everyone celebrated with exuberance and joy, those returning from the front fraternizing with those who had never been there, but had none the less waged their own battles.

And yet, even as I rejoiced at the end of the extermination of mankind among all those people crazy with joy—soldiers, Parisian men, women, children perched on their fathers' shoulders—it seemed to me that something else was also coming to an end. The war, despite all it had taken away, had given us something too—solidarity. The daily perils, the cruelties, the casualties, the difficulties of survival had, in a sense, united and integrated us all. There had been genuine friendship; people had been interested in each other and had tried to help each other by word and deed.

But peace returned us all to the society which had existed before the war, a society based on egoism, smugness, envy and boredom. The feelings of humanity and compassion for mankind and the desire to change the world and society that had been awakened by the war went back to sleep. In times of peace, most people forget how to react to the sorrows of mankind and live only for themselves, however much they may pay lip service to ideals of humanitarianism and love of their neighbour.

*　*　*

For a long time, although Diego and I no longer did anything to avoid conception, I was stricken with barrenness. It was torment to me. At the close of 1918, I obtained the address of a Russian doctor at the Cochin hospital in the rue St-Jacques, went for an examination, and was told that I was in urgent need of an operation. I knew I was suffering from the fatigues of an irregular life, but I believed that I was basically strong and healthy. I did not know what to do. I consulted Mme Savinkov, who gave me an introduction to Professor Pinard. I went to see him. He was a man advanced in years—a real 'papa'. He examined me carefully and enquired about my profession and my customary mode of life, about whether I had a lover and how he behaved in our sexual relationship. I answered all his questions and told him that at the hospital they had proposed to operate on me straight away.

Professor Pinard advised against an operation and said, 'You have a slight displacement of the womb, that is all. You are suffering from a fatigue which comes from the slightly violent character of your sexual relationship. Men are often selfish and care little for the health of their wives and mistresses. Go to bed early for a time, take great care with your intimate hygiene, and do not be too violent or passionate with your lover. You are at a fairly critical age for a woman, my dear, an age when a woman ordinarily has a fervent desire for a child. I am convinced that the child you have will be healthy and good looking—you have all the necessary stuff in you for that.'

I went out as light as a feather in the wind. For a fortnight I followed advice exactly—plenty of rest and hygiene, no amorous excesses. I felt relaxed, clear of eye and light of heart. Then came the evening when Diego and I set about, in conformity with the instructions in a Hindu book, the work of starting a baby. He told me with a laugh that if we did not succeed it would mean that the book was 'badly written'.

Diego was convinced that I was incapable of having a child, and when I told him at the beginning of March that I was pregnant he would not believe me. 'You're trying to have me on,' he said. 'Mark you, I shouldn't be sorry. Perhaps you'd leave me time to get on with my painting.'

'And with other women,' I rejoined. My gaiety had been restored. It communicated itself to Rivera and he came more often.

One splendid spring morning we set off for the Meudon woods to work. We felt young and happy, free from all our anxieties. Diego painted a water-colour lying on his back and looking at the great trees that shot up towards the sky and formed three huge green discs above his head. It was most unusual; I had never seen, or imagined one could paint, anything like it. After working we romped. I ran among the trees and Rivera tried to catch me, but I was faster.

When I let myself be caught, he strapped me to a tree, bound my hands with his neckerchief, and said, 'Now tell me the truth. No lies. Are you pregnant, yes or no?' He snapped off a small branch and began to lash my thighs and shoulders with it. His eyes flamed, and I thought it was the beginning of a fit.

And a fit it was, but of another kind. If a forest-keeper or a puritanical promenader had happened along, we should certainly have been in for a scandal and an official report, but the god of fauns and satyrs must have been watching over us. I had never seen Diego in a state like that. Drunk with nature and the sun, he behaved like a cave man.

We walked back to Paris arm in arm, and all the way he looked at me and smiled, curiously and very tenderly, and I asked myself, 'Is he pleased? Is it a joke to him? Or is it a nuisance for him?'

My whole life had recovered its colour. I was healthier, stronger, surer of myself in every way. If Diego did not come to see me when he promised to do so, I did not allow myself to be cast down to despair and wallow there. This is not to say that I did not experience violent spasms of rebellion when he neglected me immoderately or lied to me (yes, he lied—often shamelessly). Then I had recourse to blows. I remember that my landlord once saw me, from his doorway, hitting Diego with an umbrella, and told me later that I had not been striking hard enough at a man who allowed me to earn my own living in my condition.

I was working because Diego could not afford to support me. I did not expect it, nor did I want to lay claim to anything. I had obtained work through Boris Savinkov, who had placed me in his office. (I shall never forget the interest he and his wife took in me. Among my friends they were the first, with the exception of Ilya, who did not hold me up to shame.) Savinkov was a boss to dream of! He watched to see that I did not fatigue myself too much. I was supposed to be at work at nine, but I had special permission to come at ten and leave when I felt at all tired. Nobody was allowed to criticize me. If I mis-spelled names on lists or on envelopes, they were corrected quietly, without my being sworn at, as any-one else in my place would have been.

I was being paid three hundred and fifty francs a month for doing little but waste time (and how I would have enjoyed using that time to go into the country and play the fool!). Then I was given a rise of fifty francs, and I was able to buy things for Rivera that I had long dreamed of giving him—a khaki American shirt, two pairs of short drawers, socks and sock-suspenders and a lovely tie. I left them all, wrapped, with his concierge. I also bought him a pair of claret-coloured pyjamas for the evenings when he came to see me. Poor pyjamas! They shrank in the wash, as did the ones I bought for myself at the same time.

In August, at the suggestion of the Fishers (I had met them at last), Rivera took me into the country, to Lagny-sur-Marne. We lodged at a little two-storeyed house, very sunny, at the edge of a forest. The landlady was picturesque—a tiny, pink, wrinkled old woman in a blue jacket and apron and a stiff, pleated skirt, with a little white cap on her head. She cooked our meals (I helped her sometimes) and we all ate together in the garden. Diego set to work at once. I posed for him, sitting on a little bench in the cellar with my head bowed, dressed like a peasant woman. But at the end of the first picture I resigned, the protests of my child against the rigour of the pose being too lively. After that the land-lady began to sit for him in her free time, even though she had plenty to do, poor woman, with her fowls, her rabbits, her kitchen garden, her flowers and our meals!

Diego also painted landscapes, and I have a very clear memory of going to fetch him one nightfall. He was standing in the middle of the countryside like an image, his tall silhouette outlined against a sky that was still light orange; everything else was drowning in the blue-purple dusk. He did not stir, as though hypnotized by some vision. I called him very gently, and he started like someone coming out of a dream. I often helped him carry his gear back to the house, and he would tell me whether he was pleased with his work or not and ask whether I had been working too, whether I was well. We fell hungrily on the food that was waiting for us, and then I went to bed, but Diego stood for a long time looking at his canvases by the paraffin lamp or a candle and performing his nose-cleaning ritual before he would decide to go to bed. In the dark we talked quietly about colours, about composition, about ourselves, about the child. 'I didn't know it was possible to be so happy with you,' he told me.

Fate seemed to smile now that I carried within me the child I had so longed for. What confidence I had in the future! I had faith in my strength, my talent, in Diego's friendship and love, the permanence of his attachment. And he seemed to encourage my hopes. When the postman brought a letter from Angelina we read it together, and Diego would laugh at the affectionate, tender phrases it contained. 'Poor old thing!' he would say.

I pointed out that she wasn't so poor, since she still had her hooks into him. He told me that she constantly begged him not to desert her or else she would kill herself. This was sheer blackmail, and I pitied Diego for submitting to it. But perhaps at the same time that he complained to me he was complaining to Angelina that I had my hooks into him. Who knows?

He had one or two fearful paroxysms during our stay in the country. Once, in the midst of working, he crumpled up on the floor with exhaustion, his eyes white and foam on his lips. Another time, late at night, I had to run out into the garden in my nightgown and hide myself under the table. He came downstairs after me, barefooted, wearing nothing but a flapping shirt that made him look like a ghost. As usual, he was brandishing his great Mexican stick. In the moonlight, his white, upturned eyes were terrifying. He came up to the table, touched it with his stick, and said, 'Come out, *ditya*. Come out from there. I shan't hurt you'.

I had to obey, for it was dangerous to oppose him. He sniffed at me, touched my hair and said, 'I was surrounded by evil spirits and I thought I should lose you.'

I clasped him gently round the waist and led him up the stairs. He made himself heavy, like a child, but otherwise made no resistance, and he went to sleep instantly. During the night he awakened and asked me why I was not asleep. I answered that I was watching over him. It was my child too that I was watching over—I was frightened for it at such moments.

Late one night I was awakened by a noise. As I lay in the dark I heard groans coming from the old woman's room. Lighting a candle, I went to investigate, and found the old woman lying on the floor with her chamber pot beside her—clearly she had fallen off and lacked the strength to get up again. I was horrified, for Diego had been working her hard, making her pose for a picture he was painting in the Flemish style until she trembled with exhaustion. Unable to lift her, I summoned Diego, who came running in his nightshirt. We put her to bed and Diego fetched a bottle of *marc* from the kitchen and forced some of it down her throat. All the while she did not speak, merely looked at us with sorrowful eyes. We covered her up well and tiptoed out of the room.

Diego dressed hurriedly and went to the nearest house with the news that our landlady had been taken suddenly ill in the night. When he came back he said, 'Listen, *ditya*, we must get our things together and shove off as quick as we can. Her children will come and look after her. I don't want to see them with things as they are. I should have to talk—explain—No, I haven't the courage. Better to be off.'

That was Rivera all over. He was brave enough when animated by passion, but the accidents of life, the hard work of living, scared him. And so we ran away like naughty children, without telling anyone or asking for our bill.

We returned to Paris. I was now seven and a half months gone, and the most ungainly, the most painful part of my pregnancy remained. I asked Diego to find me somewhere not far from Paris where I could go to live and spend some months after my lying-in. He said he would see about it, and was as good as his word, renting for me a nice little apartment at Châtillon in the house of a pleasant widow, Madame Pite. He promised to pay the rent regularly and to come to see me twice a week. 'And I shall be able to see you at Dagusya's too,' he added.

I went to take leave of my landlord at the rue Asseline and gave him a picture and a few drawings to thank him for his kindness to me during the war years, when he would sometimes let me get as long as a year behind with the rent.

'Oh, come,' he said. 'There was nothing special in that. We had to help each other, of course. Be brave, and be more firm with your friend. Come back and see me. If I can ever do anything for you I shall be more than glad to. I've a soft spot for Russians.'

I liked my new place very much at once, although the sky was grey the day I moved in and I knew I was going to be a long way from the rue du Départ. I ordered wood and coal, energetically sawing up the wood against my return from the hospital; hard work, but there was no one else to do it. I also spent some time in the garden, where there was a delightful nanny-goat in residence.

I was exhibiting pictures that year at the Salon d'Automne, and I was determined to brave the crowds on varnishing day. I put on a roomy cloak, blue with yellow stripes and a blue velvet collar, which became me and concealed my condition, and went late in the afternoon. I met Dagusya, who told me that Diego had gone to Poitiers to study, as he had always wished to do, the tapestries and the famous stained-glass windows of the cathedral. He had left me a message that he wished to be informed of the birth of the baby by telegram.

The crowd, the jostling, the news that Diego had run away from his responsibilities (for it was nothing less)—all combined to make me giddy, and suddenly I felt violently ill. Dagusya summoned a taxi and rushed me to the Baudelocque Maternity Home in the boulevard de Port-Royal. It was already evening when we arrived, and it seemed an eternity before I was shown into an enormous ward, allocated a bed, and told to put on a nightgown and a dressing jacket of some coarse, scratchy stuff. My belongings were taken away, and from then on I was anonymous, abandoned in the middle of the ward and the women.

A kitchen attendant came by with a trolley with two great sauce-pans on it. She stopped by my bed and placed her two great red hands on her hips. 'What's this now, I wonder. Joan of Arc or a Mardi Gras get-up?'

In those days I wore my hair in long curls with a fringe on my forehead, a style which made me look like someone in an ancient fresco ('a Mantegna head,' Diego used to say).

'I've nothing for you this evening, little one. You came without notice and all the portions are accounted for.'

This was untrue. I could see quite well that there was more than enough left for me of the potato *purée* and the meat. There was also some bread left. Not content with starving me, the attendant read the card at the foot of my bed and began to berate me for being a foreigner and trying to take bed and board away from deserving Frenchwomen.

126

That was the welcome I received at the Clinique Baudelocque. My tears—tears of exhaustion, mortification, loneliness—ran onto the harsh nightgown that scratched my skin. But I knew it was too late to cry and feel sorry for myself. From now on I must think of nothing but the child.

We were awakened at six o'clock and given a laxative and allowed to wash our faces in hot water. A doctor, with whom Professor Pinard had put in a word for me, came to give me an auscultation. I admitted to him that I had sawn wood and carted heavy objects about in the last few weeks. He scolded me, and told me that the child was not quite there, even though I was beginning to lose the waters. He advised me to remain quietly in bed.

The doctor's good will toward me made a good impression on the other occupants of the ward, compensating somewhat for the enmity of the all-powerful attendant. Then Dagusya brought me an album and some crayons, and of course all the women wanted me to draw them. In the resultant portrait gallery of identically clad women, it was only by their heads and hands that the peasant, the tart, the dairy-maid and the bourgeoise could be distinguished. The doctors and nurses were interested in my drawings, and sometimes pretty nurses would come and ask me to do 'a little portrait' of them.

The days passed, and the baby did not come. Then came a day when there were no more beds free for new arrivals and I was threatened with having to give up mine. The doctor said he was sure I had made a mistake about the date and advised me to go home. This I was reluctant to do, for it was a fearfully long distance away and I was 'certain, absolutely certain' that the baby would be born in a day or two. I sent a *pneumatique* to the Savinkovs begging them to arrange for me to stay on longer at the Clinique Baudelocque.

The reply arrived after I had been dispossessed, when I was seated on a bench outside the ward, shivering with cold and apprehension. 'Keep calm. Don't stir from where you are. Everything arranged for the best. You'll be brought money too.' I felt reassured, almost happy—someone was heeding my distress. My re-entry into the ward was triumphant.

The attendant who disliked me almost chocked with chagrin. 'You're lucky, you are,' she said.

'Not me,' I said. 'It's my *baby* who's lucky.'

That was the morning of 12 November. My pains began in the evening, and I had a very bad night. The next day was the hardest time for me, and not only because of the pain. Others were talking all around me, about their earlier confinements, their illnesses and the illnesses of their children and husbands. I should have liked to be alone, in silence, to concentrate and understand what was happening inside me. There are those who say that childbirth is an ugly performance; they also say that a pregnant woman is ugly. But I have always considered a birth to be something beautiful and miraculous.

My child was born between seven and eight in the evening of 13 November, the very date Diego had wished for (he himself had been born on 13 November). It was a girl: very tiny.

'A little frog,' the doctor said. 'Do you want to hold her and suckle her? See how little she is and how she needs you.'

I saw. With all my strength, with all my flesh, with all my mind I already loved this child that I had so desperately desired, like a joy, a miracle, an absolution for my past life. I remembered the ecstasy I had felt at carrying it within me, in spite of so many difficulties and sorrows. In the garden at Châtillon I had sung and danced for happiness, all alone, free to conjure up Diego and his love for me in my imagination. That was what had sustained me, that and the country air and the longing of my soul that Diego should love the child I was carrying as I loved it.

Would things have turned out differently if I had given him a child earlier in our relationship?

My daughter's first visitors were Dagusya and Fisher, and the moment they saw the cluster of newly born babies they recognized her, for she resembled her father so much. Among so many cherubic pink babies, her slightly greenish pallor, her little forehead covered with hair, her eyes, her rather swollen mouth proclaimed her a being apart. There was nothing French or Slavonic about her, and everyone soon called her 'Diega, the little Mexican.'

Rivera came the day after the child's birth. He approached my bed, nervous and ill at ease, trying to hide a little bouquet behind his back. I was suddenly reminded that Angelina had had a room of her own; reminded also of the two big bouquets of long ago, one for her and one for me. As I looked at this giant, with his huge hat and enormous, parti-coloured stick, swaying on his flat feet among all these women's beds, I wondered what obscure power had bound us to each other.

'He's a Mexican, and she's Russian. . . . Artists. . . .' I heard the whispers clearly.

The baby was so small that it was feared she could not suck and would have to be put in the incubator. But the nurse put a finger into the little mouth to make it bigger, and I offered my breast. The baby began to suck at once, the milk came, all went well.

It was otherwise with the christening arrangements. Diego did not offer to acknowledge his daughter, and I was too proud to ask him, so when I was asked what name the child was to bear I gave mine and my father's, 'Vorobëv-Stebelska' (but on the birth certificate they put 'daughter of Vorobëv and Stebelsky'—the kind of accident that often happens with such papers. I believed that I had done all that was necessary to have my daughter acknowledged, and persuaded myself that later on Diego would put everything in order. (Six or seven years later, I was told that my daughter had neither father nor mother because I had not filled out the proper form, stamped, in front of two witnesses. I saw to it then, of course, but I am still vexed at the negligence which allowed me to leave the maternity home so completely ignorant of French law in 1919.)

I left the Clinique Baudelocque with a thousand francs on me, sent by Boris Savinkov (Savinkov, in fact, did more for me at this time than Diego, who did not pay for my confinement, as I found out when I was dunned for the money later). Diego came for me and we took a taxi to Châtillon, where a fire was waiting for us. I put the baby into a little cradle and told Rivera that I was suckling Marika myself.

'You named her Marika?'

'You used to call me that, didn't you? I've called her the same. It's very pretty.'

That was all.

Marika put him out of temper. I often had the sense that the child and I were disturbing him, either in his work or some amorous adventure, and yet, God knows, it was little enough time he devoted to us. One day, in a rage, he gripped my throat and squeezed—hard. Suddenly the baby started crying and he let go.

'She's saved you,' he said.

'What have I done? You neglect me, you do nothing for the child. I'm not demanding anything from you—except your presence here now and again. If you still love me, show it. If you don't, give me your friendship, your moral support. I need you badly just now.'

He went away, still raging.

Sometimes I got a *pneumatique* to say he was not coming; sometimes he came without notice.

The spring came. When Diego was there we were happy. We went for long walks and chattered away as before. But a new element had entered our life. I fretted. Diego was giving us only a hundred and fifty francs a month, and there was the rent, wood, coal, food, not to mention fluctuating expenses like water, gas, electricity, medicines. I was tormented with the idea that my milk was not rich enough for my child.

A time came when Diego did not appear for six days. Mme Pite advised me to go to Paris to see what had become of him, and since I had not a penny she lent me enough for the return fare by tram.

I waited in the rue du Départ till midday, but saw no sign of Diego. I summoned all my courage and went into the house, climbed the stairs to the door marked 'Diego Rivera—Angelina Beloff'. I knocked. The door was opened by Angelina, who turned scarlet when she saw me.

'I should like to see Rivera,' I said. 'It's almost a week since he's been to see us. I've no more money. I can't work and. . . .

'He's not in. How dare you come here?' And she slammed the door in my face so hard that the baby began to whimper.

Seething with rage and humiliation, I went to a square close by and fed the baby. Then I saw Diego striding towards the house. I called his name. When he saw me, he jumped as though he had had an electric shock.

'All these days I've been meaning to drop in or write, Marevna. But I'm frightfully busy, you know. Why have you come?'

'To see whether you weren't ill, and also because I haven't a penny. Mme Pite lent me the money to come. What am I to do, Diego? I don't want to parade my poverty. Perhaps you can't give me more than you do. Perhaps you're robbing yourself as it is. But the baby, yours and mine. Look at her—isn't she lovely? Are you frightened of Angelina and the scenes she makes? I've just seen her, and she slammed the door in my face.'

'You did that? You went up with the baby?'

'Yes. I don't think I could ever have been so cruel. If she'd come to me with her child I'd have been glad to open my door to a woman—a woman of *yours*, Diego—who was knocking to ask for help. It's not entirely my fault, you know, that I've no money. And Mme Pite wants her rent. How wretched it all is!'

Looking uncomfortable, smiling a little vacantly, he promised to send Dagusya with some money the next day. He promised as well to come soon himself.

What could I do? The illness and death of little Diego lived in my memory. I refused to sacrifice my daughter, and I had to resign myself for the moment to the petitioner's role. Things were bound to improve, I told myself. Diego would come back to me and would love his daughter in spite of all the women around him, in spite of Angelina. I went back to Châtillon.

Dagusya came next morning with the promised money, and told me that Rivera was mad with anger at my going to see Angelina. She also told me that she herself had gone to the apartment shortly after I left and found Angelina rolling on the floor in hysterics. She had shouted that she wanted to throw herself out of the window, and when Rivera came in had actually tried to do so.

I protested that this was only a pretence, an attempt to trade on Diego's weakness and cowardice and keep him from abandoning her. I said that many times I had felt a desire to throw myself and the baby under a lorry in despair at his weakness. 'He can't call his soul his own, Dagusya. In order to have peace, and a little out of charity, he consents to lead this life. He deceives her, and she consents to it—so long as I'm not the other woman. She hates me, wishes I and my baby were dead. Don't think ill of me, Dagusya. I'm only asking for a little pity for the baby. You don't know how terrible it can be to know that tomorrow there will be nothing to eat and that that means I shan't have my milk. Why should the baby suffer for the sins of her father, her mother and a woman who hates her? And don't try to talk to me about Angelina's sufferings! If she'd looked after her son decently. . . . And Marika's only five months old. What will become of her a few months from now?'

Dagusya was a good soul, but she had taken Angelina's side. Angelina might not be Rivera's legal wife, but in the eyes of the world, for all my sincerity, for all my poverty, I was the intruder, the adventuress. I had chosen solitude and freedom—the hard path.

The days passed and Diego did not appear. The baby looked magnificent. I put her out naked in the sunshine, and she was gilded all over. She grew. She was solid. Fisher, who often visited us, took a photograph of her—a small parcel of brown flesh that was the image of Diego.

One day Fisher told me that Diego had at last agreed to acknowledge the child. The very next morning, I was to get the child ready and I would be fetched. I was overjoyed. I had not broached the subject to Diego because of the ugly scene following his discovery that I had given the child my name; furious, he had accused me of not being sure he was the father and I had accused him of behaving despicably. Now, I thought, his conscience (with assistance from the Fishers) was prompting him to do right.

No one came to fetch us the next morning. I learned later from Fisher that at the last moment Diego had backed out.

I found work with the Red Cross in Paris, sewing shirts and drawers for the wounded and for prisoners, but I had not the experience to earn more than two or three francs a day. Then I hit on an idea. I possessed a lovely Russian bridle, woven in several colours, that I wore as a belt. Why not try to copy it and sell the result? I fastened several lengths of thread to the hasp of the window as a warp and set to work, producing a pretty belt decorated with tufts of wool. I made several more, varying the colours and design. A neighbour thought them charming and bought two. I took the rest to Paris, and everyone liked them. I began to get orders, and before long I was earning between four and five hundred francs a month—enough to dress the growing child and myself and buy what I needed for my work without giving up the country air. Or my freedom—I could sing, shout, weep, and nobody had the right to say anything.

Meanwhile, Diego did not come near me, and seeing this, the pleasant Mme Pite became increasingly unpleasant. For her I was only a sinner, an unmarried mother, and she began to show her disapproval of my way of life. I took other lodgings at Châtillon in the middle of a big garden of fruit trees, shrubbery, and kitchen garden. I had no bathroom and no electricity, but the rent was low and the certainty of being alone made up for the lack of comfort. I moved in towards the end of September, and the next day I ran round the garden with the baby in my arms, well-wrapped up because it was very cold. There were birds cheeping 'puic-puic-puic' on the bare branches of the trees, and Marika thought this very funny. Gradually, I began to think it was still possible to be happy.

Marika was learning to walk and talk. This is to say she jumped and stamped in one spot and uttered her first words, which usually all sounded like 'bla-bla' or 'cra-cra'.

On the evening of Christmas Day, when I was delightedly watching the thirteen-month-old Marika's ecstasies over the tree with its lighted candles and the presents I had made for her, there was a knock on the door. The thought flashed through my mind that perhaps Christmas had brought back the penitent papa, as

133

happens in the tales.

Indeed, there he was, with Dagusya. (Ironic that she, who once had pulled my leg unmercifully over my 'orang-outang', had now become his page.) He had brought a big plush monkey, and Marika was in raptures, though rather intimidated by Diego's beard and his bulk. They thought she was charming and looked very healthy.

The purpose of their visit was to inform me that Diego, following a journey to Italy, intended to return to Mexico. Would I consent to entrust Marika to him, allow him to take his daughter to his homeland, where his parents were still living? The question was put to me by Dagusya casually, between sips of tea.

The news of his departure was in itself a blow to make me tremble. But let him take my child away from me? 'Take us both with you,' I implored him. 'I'm losing you. I can't let her go as well. She's too small. I'd have to be sure she's going to live. I'd have to devote two or three years to her. I'm ready to go with you as nurse, that's all—for Marika's sake.'

'Now, now, *ditya*, you have your work,' Diego said. 'You don't want to be a wet-nurse all your life.' He urged me to think it over during the time he was in Italy and, as he was leaving, he whispered to me that he would return the following afternoon.

My spirits soared. From the way his glistening eyes had looked at me all evening, I realized that all these months without a sight of me had reawakened his sexual curiosity. I was not mistaken. When he reappeared it was obvious that he felt newly attracted to me.

'Do you know you've changed a lot, *ditya*? I believe that now I could make something of you.'

We talked as we had talked in the past, about our work, about our aspirations. He asked me how I managed to live without painting. I told him that my earnings and the money he gave me covered only my bare subsistence and that of the child. How could I paint without canvases or paints?

He was affectionate, passionate. His presence warmed my heart and ignited in me again the hope of a better future.

'Listen, Marevna, when I leave for Mexico I shan't be able to take you with me. I shan't have enough money. But when I'm there, if all goes as I want and hope, I'll write to you and send you money, and you'll come with the child. Or why not give her to me when I go? And you shall come afterwards, I swear.'

I asked nothing better than to believe his promises. But part with my daughter? No.

The weeks passed. I worked in the garden and loved it, though at first if an earthworm came up out of the ground I would drop my spade and flee, shuddering. My neighbours laughed and begged me to collect the worms to feed their hens, so I overcame my repugnance and in exchange received good advice about gardening.

My peas and onions were coming up, the whole garden was flowering, including the shrubbery, and Marika was playing with a rabbit someone had given her on the morning the tall, heavy form came through the garden gate. I suppressed an impulse to run and throw my arms around his neck and let him come up to me. He had changed. He had shaved all the hair off his face and looked vastly younger, but I preferred him with his beard, which gave his face more character and concealed a receding chin.

'I always find you in excellent form when I come back,' he said.

'A good sign. And I'm always glad to see you again.'

We were about to kiss, but suddenly Marika started stamping her foot and uttering piercing screams.

'Look at that!' said Diego. 'Jealousy, or I know nothing about women. Where does she get that from, I wonder?'

He showed me some splendid drawings of women he had made in Italy. I could see that his art had developed, and I was happy.

'I did them in a brothel,' he said. 'The women were glad to pose. Oh, nothing dirty or obscene, you know. No, it was natural, powerful, beautiful—like love itself.'

We acquired fresh knowledge of each other. It was all beginning anew . . .

Rivera had come back at a good time. I could cook *my* peas for him and *my* new potatoes. (They were tiny. I did not yet know how to grow vegetables properly. But what did it matter?) Marika began to get used to her father, and he to her. If the child was disobedient and I reprimanded her, Diego would say, 'Don't listen to your mother—she's a fool,' and I began to think that if this went on I should have my work cut out for me. He would perch her on his shoulders, dancing a Mexican dance and singing a Mexican song. She thought she had a right to all his attention, and would often go into a tantrum if he came near me, much less touched me. Sometimes he would make a drawing of her; sometimes I sat too for a drawing or a water-colour. My stock went up with the neighbours when they saw I was not neglected by my child's father, and from seeing him nicer and kindlier than ever, I gained a measure of security. We spoke no more of the journey to Mexico, and I allowed myself to hope that the plan had been abandoned.

One day, however, he arrived with the news that his father was very ill, and he must make haste or perhaps lose the chance of seeing him again alive. 'You wish me to go, don't you, *ditya*?'

What woman in such circumstances would have said no? I bit back all my protests and swallowed my tears. I lifted the baby in my arms and said that at all events I should still have something of him to console me. He caressed her and wept as I tucked her into bed.

'I swear to you that as soon as things improve I'll send for you and the child, Marevna. I shan't forget the two of you, little Marika and big Marika.'

He made passionate love to me for the last time. Smothering my hands and lips with kisses, he begged me, as a last favour, not to come to the station next day. (Was he afraid that I would make a public scene, parade my martyrdom with the baby in my arms?) The bitterness and salt of tears were mingled with our kisses, for this time I wept too, perhaps less over Diego's going than over the thought of what was to become of little Marika.

I let him go too easily. Counting on my own strength and on his fondness for me, I still hoped in my heart of hearts that one day everything would turn out for the best. If I had foreseen how unhappy my daughter would be, I would have insisted, cost what it might, on his acknowledging her before he went. When a love affair is over there is nothing to be done about it, but when one leaves children behind, one must think of their destiny, their future. Marika was intelligent and sensitive—too sensitive. She grew up in the midst of a perpetual whispering. 'She has no father. . . . Her father and mother weren't married. . . . Her father never acknowledged her. . . .' In spite of all my efforts to bring it home to her that this was a common occurrence among artists, I saw her wound grow more painful, I saw her retire into herself and develop a kind of grudge against her father and me.

Before he departed for Mexico, Rivera left several thousand francs with Fisher, with instructions to give me some regularly every month. This was very nice of him. Also, when Marika was two and about to undergo an appendectomy, I wrote to him, begging him to help, and he did. In the letter that accompanied the money, he wrote that while our child was ill his father had expired in his arms after a long illness. He avowed his affection for Marika (and I believed from the tone of the letter that this was no lie), expressed his sorrow at her illness and begged me to send him frequent news of her. He went on to say that he had loving memories of me, and that his work would always bear the stamp of the glorious days he had spent in Paris, thanks to me.

Neither this letter nor the one that followed contained any mention of plans for Marika and me. Reading between the lines, I divined that he was in the grip of a new love affair. 'I can't work if I am not madly in love with a woman. As at the time when I met you and was like a madman (and it was reflected in my painting) so now I can again devote myself entirely to my work.' In fact it was at this time that he fell in love with Lupe Marin, whom he married.

I answered that I understood perfectly, and begged him not to forget us altogether. I told him that I often talked about him to his daughter, in order that she might continue to love him even from far away.

After this I received nothing more from him.

What remains to be said about Diego Rivera? He was far from

admirable in many ways, unquestionably. To satisfy his burning passion for love-making and women—all women—he was capable of any folly. Later, when he began a new life of commitment in Mexico, he was no more faithful to his Communist party than to his women, deserting it twice and returning in penitence. Perhaps it is wrong to judge him as a man, for he was an artist before anything else. All questions of conscience and duty came a distant second to his painting.

Where his work was concerned, Rivera was strong, and did not hesitate to pursue the direction he thought right for himself. In Europe his work was uncertain, groping, showing the influences of the Spanish school—Velazquez, El Greco, Goya (whom he greatly resembled, both physically and in his mode of living)—and the French school—Cézanne, the douanier Rousseau, Picasso, Gris, Braque. He fell out with almost all his cubist friends when he abandoned Cubism, as he might have abandoned a woman from whom he had taken everything, saying, 'Cubism is excellent, but only as a means. It is not the true goal.' He quarrelled with Rosenberg almost as soon as their contract was signed, but if Rosenberg hoped that Rivera would come begging to be taken back he was wrong. The true road to fame Rivera found in Mexico. In his murals, which made him famous as a fresco painter all over the world, he displayed all his love, all his passion for his country and his people. Everything he had learned in Europe, in Paris, served him as a means of achieving a personal artistic language, full of passion and colour.

It is almost a commonplace that the faults of the man should not be held against the artist. But I greatly regret that later in his career Rivera made certain compromises, largely because his entourage was not always wholesome. Too many women—that is what I reproach him with.

A short time after Rivera left Paris, I went one day to the Montrouge cemetery (it was one of his last requests to me that I should), and had the greatest difficulty finding the grave of his little son. It was overgrown; the white cross was worm-eaten; the word 'Diego' was barely discernible. I asked Fisher to give me some of Rivera's money to pay the rent for the plot and have the grave tidied up.

'Let the dead boy be, Marevna,' Fisher said. 'Think first of your daughter who's alive. It's Angelina's business to see to it, but she's not interested any more.'

III
Soutine : an appreciation

Soutine: an appreciation

I have already mentioned that Soutine and I were drawn together by our love of nature and our ability to see fantastic shapes in everything around us. Both of us found inspiration for our work in our childhood memories.

Soutine's childhood world was a Grand Guignol world of nightmarish shapes, grimaces, cries of protest and rebellion. In his realistic, simplified forms the prevailing element is always fantasy; sometimes tragic, sometimes childishly comical. His paintings are full of deep, mysterious shadows and lines crossing each other to form triangles and spheres. Everything leads a life of its own. His portraits, consciously or unconsciously depicting those who peopled his childhood, conjure up before us a Guignol theatre, in which the actors in the comedy of life pose in tragi-comic masks and attitudes. In the landscapes everything bends over and whirls, and seems to be running and dancing; his trees are not trees, and his dead birds are not birds. Horror and violent death are here in abundance. His work arouses feelings of anxiety, and one is visually uneasy when looking at some of his paintings.

But behind this ugly façade of Soutine's fantastic art we can see too the other side of the enchanted world of people, birds, objects and nature itself—his deep love of life, like that of Cézanne and Courbet. Soutine once told me that in the summer, when he was angry with his father, he would take a piece of bread and an onion (a great sin!) and run off to the fields, where he would sleep in a herdsman's hut, or to the forest, where he would climb a tree, settle himself comfortably, and spend hours watching and listening to forest life. He watched the rich colours of the foliage and the crimson and golden rays of the setting sun through the dark branches; he listened to the noise of the wind, the calling of birds, the hooting of owls, and was lulled to sleep, breathing in the fresh fragrance of the forest. Sometimes he was joined by a companion in his escapades; this was more amusing, but lessened the enchantment of the forest. Listening to Soutine, I thought of the great physical and moral benefits that those evenings and nights in field and forest must have brought him; for there he could have respite from his home life and be enriched by impressions healthier than those of the village of Smilovichi, where there was neither the peace nor the time to devote himself to quiet observation.

Soutine, like Courbet, loved to paint forests, and painted them with great animation and fantasy. He painted trees, branches and foliage with thick strokes, as Van Gogh did at the beginning of his career. He painted with brushes and then with brush handles, making arabesques in the branches and scratches here and there. His trees are alive. These giants, agitated by the wind, wave their branches like arms and stride forward on both sides of a road, along which two small boys, holding hands, are pattering, perhaps on their way home from school. The storm is over, and the wind is driving the last thunderclouds across the clearing sky. Some of the trees stand like sentinels, bowed in thought over a dark pool; others are caught up in a round dance with the wind, bending left and then right, surrounded by a dense crowd of curious companions. All this emerged from Soutine's distant childhood. The little boys are himself and a brother, or friends running hungry from school to the village. The storm has caught them in the wood, frightening them quite a bit, and the rain has drenched them. But now the wind is hurrying them on and drying their clothes, while the friendly trees are running after them, making fun of them, gently tapping them with wet branches. The setting sun is sparkling in the rain puddles. The rain-heavy corn is gradually straightening up on either side of the road, beckoning with its poppies and cornflowers, and the playful, piercing cries of swallows sound in their ears.

Discussions of a painter's work often boil down to the question of whether or not he can draw. Modigliani loved drawing, and used to say that it was as essential for the painter as singing is for birds and water for fish. But there are some excellent painters who never drew, but painted directly on the canvas, and Soutine is one of them. Some critics appraise works of art solely according to the manner in which they are created. In my opinion, however, skill is not enough. I think that an artist must also have a divine spark, that is to say, talent and also a genuine love of art, of painting and of everything that surrounds us: I mean, of course, love of life.

* * *

The Polish painter, Zborowski, the patron of Soutine, Modigliani, Kisling and others, was a good man and a good friend to his painters. He wanted to make them into great artists, but when he and his wife became dealers they were forced, like all dealers, to become materialists, and he worked his painters hard. Sometimes he would lock one of them up in a room with cigarettes, a litre of wine and some sandwiches until a picture was finished. This worked well enough with Modi, who would often produce a picture in two or three days—even in one day—under those conditions. But with Soutine this method was dangerous, for he would not submit to being coerced and became ill or lost control of himself and in fury and desperation smashed everything in sight.

In 1919 Zborowski sent Soutine to Céret in the Eastern Pyrenees, where the painter's work gained force and sureness. There he evolved the basic style which he was to use for the rest of his life. Céret was a haven of quiet, a mysterious temple of nature. Picasso had been there much earlier, with his wife and Max Jacob; the poet had painted water-colours, and the painter had written poetry. In 1911 Picasso had returned to Céret with

145

Soutine and Zborowsky

Georges Braque, and they had worked together. Another dis-
coverer of the village was Pinchus Kremègne, who, having spent
much time there over the years, has now settled there. After four
years spent under bombardment in Paris, where every new day
had threatened catastrophe, where everyone was half-starved,
where in winter everyone shivered for lack of coal, Soutine
revived in Céret and got on his feet again. The mountain folk
were peaceable and friendly, smilingly saluting the pale, sickly
Parisian; they were not frightened by him or by his art: but perhaps, after Picasso's paintings, Soutine's seemed to them mere
childish dabs. The healthy mountain air and the good food im-

146

pelled the painter towards fresh creative effort. Newly awakened forces churned within him.

But the feeling of fear experienced in Paris, the resentment and protest against the war erupted in his work. If we look at his output in Céret, we come to the inescapable conclusion that something was going on inside him then which he had never before experienced. On his canvases, he constructed and reconstructed landscapes, reconstructed nature itself. In these landscapes, everything is in a whirl, in motion. Soutine gave his imagination free rein and painted not only with his mind, but with his inner self, with a kind of supernatural force. Sometimes it seems as though he had worked under the influence of drugs, as Modi and Jacob used to do—all this fantasy, this extraordinary imagery, this passion are akin to narcotic dreams. Perhaps Céret did indeed act like a drug on the young artist who had come through the war in Paris. He spent time in Céret from 1919 to 1922, and it is, indeed, a pity that he never went back to the place which helped him to find the form and line of his landscape composition. One critic has written that Soutine's Céret style combines Expressionism with Abstract Art. Perhaps this was true for a time, but Soutine loved life and nature and its forms too much to embrace the abstract entirely.

Zborowski also sent Soutine to Cagnes-sur-mer, a village with curious lanes of imbricated shingles and houses of the fourteenth, fifteenth and sixteenth centuries, picturesquely scattered over a hill overgrown with pines, olive trees and scented herbs and descending all the way down to the coast. At that time Cagnes was populated mainly by fishermen, farmers and labourers, but artists were drawn there from all over, following the lead of Auguste Renoir, who had abandoned Paris to live there on a small but very attractive estate, 'Les Collets'. Soutine went there for the first time in 1918, and thereafter for months of every year between 1918 and 1925. Zborowski favoured the Mediterranean atmosphere in order that Soutine should paint pictures in the gay colours of the Côte d'Azur, which could be sold more easily.

Although the Mediterranean had a calming effect on Soutine

because of its mild climate and its colours resembling those of the Italian primitives, painting in soft red, pink, yellow and blue shades did not suit his nature, for he had periods of extraordinary turbulence and violence. Nevertheless, he painted some splendid pictures at Cagnes, in the rue Louis Barri and the rue St Gothard. His Cagnes landscapes represent hills overgrown with tall, dark trees and studded with golden-yellow houses, which clamber up the hills on top of one another from base to summit, while narrow, winding roads either slope down or climb uphill. Whereas Soutine's Céret landscapes are constructed on the basis of diagonals, he often depicted Cagnes under the influence of Bonnard and Cézanne, placing the landscape in one or two spheres, with pyramids and angles, and a few of the pictures show a cubist influence. All the structural lines of spheres or triangles flow together, so that everything is 'in motion, dancing, circling and inclining,' to quote critics, and all this lives a life of its own, because Soutine knew how to harmonize the structural plan of his paintings with the forms of nature. His paintings of dark hill cypresses approaches Van Gogh and his mastery of representation: the cypresses sway before the mistral, their branches surging and waving in the wind.

Modigliani and Kisling also spent time in Cagnes, and for a while Modi and Soutine lived and worked together. The friendship between the two was deep and enduring, marked by devotion on both sides. Soutine adored Modi, who on his side felt great compassion for the most wretched and ill of all the emigré artists in Paris and admired the energy, self-denial and sacrifice that Soutine expended on the work he loved above all else. The two gave each other the mutual sustenance of their talent and spiritual strength, that Picasso and Max Jacob had shared together. I, too, had known the rewards of living and working with another artist when I worked in Rivera's studio.

In 1920 Modigliani died in a Paris hospital. I saw him shortly before the end in Montparnasse, when he had just come back from Cagnes. He told me that he was then getting a monthly allowance of three thousand francs from Zborowski and that his wife was pregnant. 'I'm getting fat and becoming a respectable citizen at Cagnes-sur-mer. I'm going to have two kids. It's unbelievable. It's sickening!'

He looked well, none the less. It was after his return to Paris that he fell seriously ill and died at the age of thirty-six, his premature death, generally speaking, the result of his feckless life. Everyone knows what 'bohemianism' is, and Modi, who had been weakly since childhood, unstintingly abused his strength and energy with alcohol and such harmful drugs as hashish and cocaine. Also, he loved his work and strained himself over its execution—strained himself with passion and to excess.

Modigliani's wife (his third and last love) had left the security of a good bourgeois French family, impelled by a desire to paint, and strayed to Montparnasse, where she had fallen in with the dazzling, dangerous Modi—too late for him, unfortunately. Jeanne Hébuterne, 'Haricot Rouge,' as the girl was nicknamed, was beautiful, all sweetness and gentleness; I can see her now in a clinging green frock, with a black velvet hat on her head. I knew her well, and once she sat for me for a portrait, which I painted in the cubist manner (I do not know what became of it). After Modi's funeral, she threw herself out of a fourth-floor window. She was then more than eight months gone with her second child.

For my part, I know few tales so shocking as that of Modigliani. It is frightful that such a great talent could have been, during his lifetime, so neglected and unrecognized. In return for a glass of wine, Modi would make anyone a present of a drawing, done anywhere, at any time of day or night. I had several—portraits of myself, of Rivera, or of Modi himself—and in my turn made presents of them to friends. Once the artist was dead, the boom was on, and any specimens of his work (including forgeries) commanded high prices. I had the bizarre experience of being offered a drawing of myself, which I had given away years earlier—for a mere thirty thousand francs!

The death of Modigliani was a great loss to Soutine and a cause of much suffering. Moreover, suddenly he had to pull himself together. He, too, had learned to drink a great deal in his student years in Vilna and in Paris, where wine was cheap and some cafés stayed open all night, so that he could sit till morning drinking and talking about art. Discussions and arguments about art aroused thirst, which had to be quenched, and as this in turn encouraged further talk, further argument, yet, further drink. Soutine's great misfortune was that he neither knew how to drink nor could he take drink. Although spirits and wine at first stimulated his energies, he would afterwards be laid out flat and be unable to work. His liver, his stomach, his whole sick body, undermined from childhood, revolted against the abuse of alcohol.

Rivera introduced Soutine to Dr Elie Faure, who became very interested in him, both as a man and as an artist (Rivera told me that the doctor regarded Soutine as a unique and extremely gifted painter, prophesying great fame for him). Dr Faure subsequently wrote a book about Soutine, in which he stated that the painter suffered from epilepsy (as did Rivera) and that he was sterile. Soutine was strictly forbidden by Dr Faure to drink spirits or to eat such spicy foods as pickled gherkins, cabbage and herrings— in short, everything that Russians and Jews like to eat. Soutine would reluctantly drink milk for a few days until a crisis had passed, and would then start to consume large quantities of wine and *marc* again. 'Milk makes me sick,' he would say, grimacing.

Zborowski sent his artists away from Paris and its alluring *bistros*; but, unfortunately, temptation is present everywhere. Then, too, a painter, who is obliged—come what may—to complete a certain number of landscapes and still-lifes within a given period, even when his creative capacity is temporarily at a low ebb, endures the fatigue of a treadmill donkey. Soutine was a sick man who worked as though he were healthy, at a frenzied pace, until he could work no more. Taking into account his frail constitution— his digestion, his liver, his fits and his weak left eye—we can readily understand his nervous condition and his frequent spells of hysteria, in which he not only scraped the paint off his unsuccessful canvases, but even went so far as to destroy them by cutting them up or trampling on them. These spells continued even after his period at Céret, where his inspiration was not dulled, but on the contrary flourished. The fever which came over him in the Pyrenees was the astounding fever of creative force, and it abated gradually, becoming less turbulent.

After leaving Céret, Soutine began to paint more peacefully. But it was characteristic of his creative processes for him to fall into apathy at times, as he did at Cagnes, from which he took all he could for his art before the very nature of the Mediterranean, the *dolce far'niente*, overcame him. During his stay there in 1923 he worked lifelessly; he was dispirited and bored, and wrote his famous letter to Zborowski in which he begged permission to return to Paris. The letter is a cry from the heart of an artist stifling in the atmosphere of a little place of which he was tired, and which no longer met his moral and artistic needs.

Dear Zborowski.

I have received the letter and the money order. Thank you very much. I am sorry I haven't written to you before about my work. This is the first time that I have not been able to do anything. I am in a bad state of mind. I am demoralized, and this has affected my work. I have done only seven canvases. I am sorry about this. I wanted to leave Cagnes, this landscape which I cannot stand any more. I even went for a few days to Cap Martin, where I thought I would settle. I did not like it, and I had to paint over some pictures I had begun.

I am back in Cagnes, against my will. Instead of landscapes, I shall have to do some wretched still-lifes.

You will understand what a state of indecision I am in.

Couldn't you tell me of a place to go, as on several occasions I had intended to go back to Paris.

Yours Soutine
7 rue Louis Barri, Cagnes
1923

* * *

One day in the winter of 1922–23, I ran into a highly excited Zborowski in the street. 'Do you know what's happened? Something extraordinary! For a long time now I haven't been able to find a single serious buyer for our Soutine. And after all, I'm not a millionaire, and just think how much Modi cost me—although

151

he's going uphill now. But I was really in despair about Soutine. All these gifted "daubs" of his horrify most people, and very few believe in his great talent. A day or two ago I had a quarrel with my wife, took a batch of Soutine's pictures, stripped them off their sub-frames, rolled up the lot and shoved them in the kitchen stove to burn them. "To hell with them!" I thought. The next day—just listen to this—suddenly I get a visit from the famous American collector, Dr Barnes, who just happens to be passing through Paris. "What have you got that's new? Show me," he says, and I show him Kislings, Modiglianis and so on. "And what's this?" he asks, pointing to a little painting of Soutine's on the wall. "Oh," I say, "it's by some wretched Russian." "Bring it to the light," he says, and examines it from all angles. "Any more of these?" he asks. "Yes," I say, "just wait a moment, I'll run across to a friend who has some." Then I dash to the kitchen in a cold sweat, wondering if the cook's burned up the pictures or not. I open the stove—thank God, no! Wonderful! I heat the iron and iron out a few creases through a cloth, and then I produce a living soul for this American—not my own soul, you understand, but Soutine's.

'Well, Barnes examines the paintings for a long time—puts one canvas after another up on the table, tells me to hold them up against the wall so he can view them from a distance, screws up his eyes to peer at them, looks at them through his fist, in a little mirror—Finally, he says, "I'll take everything. Tell this Soutine to work for me for a year or two, and then we'll see." Well, we do some calculations and draw up a paper, all in proper order, and now Chaim Soutine's career is in the bag. In a year or two he'll have an exhibition in Paris, and then in America. With good publicity, you'll see our Soutine become a very successful painter. How could I have doubted it, idiot that I am! You know, Marevna, I'm as glad as if I were Soutine himself.' And indeed, Zborowski was beaming.

Soon after this, Soutine began to live better and to feel more buoyant. But he had to work unremittingly for the American, to the detriment of his creative capacity.

In 1927 Paul Guillaume arranged an exhibition of Soutine's

Céret landscapes in a small gallery in the rue du Faubourg St Honoré. The place was badly lit, and the pictures were hung too closely together. This created a dazzling effect, especially where there was a preponderance of red—a colour of which Soutine was particularly fond. 'Ah, how he sloshes it about! Doesn't spare the paint, does he? He plasters it on as if he were smearing on *kissel*,' came a Russian whisper, full of envy and delight. Soutine used thick, viscous brush strokes to convey movement, and these masses of paint, looking as if they had been flung onto the canvases, had an extraordinary force. One approached close to the pictures, craning one's neck to see those overhead, and felt not only the painter's strength, talent and colour sense, but above all his vivid imagery. Most of those present were artists, many of them Russians, collectors and art-lovers, but there were also passers-by who had dropped in casually and stood there open-mouthed and uncomprehending, finally stalking out with an indignant 'Modern art is no good!' And yet a forceful talent burgeoned out of the simple frames, as did an extraordinary imagination.

That same year my friend Pierre Loeb, on learning that I had known Soutine for a long time, suggested that I should ask him to paint my portrait or my daughter Marika's. 'If he paints it, I'll buy it from you straight away for twenty thousand francs. That's money, you know. You could go south, to the seaside.' By then it was common knowledge that Soutine was going uphill (Rivera, Zborowski and Dr Faure had not been mistaken in their judgment of his work), but Loeb's idea did not attract me, largely because I should have wanted to keep such a portrait, had I had one. Moreover, Soutine and I had not met for some time, both of us being busy with our own concerns.

Then one day in the summer of 1927, coming out of the Edgar Quinet Métro near where we lived, eight-year-old Marika and I found ourselves face to face with Soutine. He greeted me effusively. 'What a long time it's been since we've seen each other, Marevna! How good to meet you like this! Is this your daughter? So that's what she's like! You know, she's very like her father, only beautiful, and she's like you too, only her eyes aren't blue, they're grey with big black irises. Come and have tea at my place. We can't just part again. perhaps for another few years. I live quite near here.'

His house was not far from the Métro. The studio and kitchen, facing onto the Boulevard Edgar Quinet, were on the ground floor, and a staircase led up to the bedroom, another room and a bathroom stacked with all kinds of rubbish. I was immediately struck by the lack of comfort, the disorder and the smell of stale tobacco in the stuffy rooms.

So was Marika. 'Look, Mama, what a mess he has here! Give me a broom and I'll clear things up for you. How can he ask guests into such a place? A real rubbish heap!' She found a broom and, wasting no time, chattering away in French, she started sweeping the studio floor and picking up cigarette ends, newspapers, pieces of torn pictures, bottles and medicine phials. 'You know, Soutine, we have a studio too, oh, much much bigger than yours, and two terraces, and a Siamese cat—a lovely one! You know, sometimes when I scream at Mama, the cat comes and takes my nose in her mouth and puts her front paws on my cheeks, and her claws are two centimetres long! Oh, she's a monster, but she doesn't scratch, and she loves music. And you, Soutine, do you live alone?'

'What a girl you've got there, Marevna,' said Soutine, smilingly watching Marika as she bustled around.

'Haven't you got a daughter, a wife, or a *femme de ménage*?' Marika persisted, raising so much dust that we had to open the studio door leading out onto the boulevard. 'Look, there's a whole chemist's shop here. Are you ill or something?'

'My stomach and liver are out of order,' said Soutine, 'and I don't like *femmes de ménage*. They're always gossiping, always touching things they shouldn't and they want to know everything. At one time, when I used to throw torn canvases into the dustbin, the *femme de ménage* used to fish them out and sell them to fanciers of my work, and they'd mend them, sign them with my name, and sell them! I managed to catch one of them at it. Imagine, it was one of my friends, but he was down on his luck so I forgave him.

154

Now I burn my unsuccessful pictures. No, I don't trust *femmes de ménage*—and I can't stand them!'

'Ah, Soutine, I can see you're not an easy person. But you know, Mama isn't fond of them either.'

'And she isn't fond of talking, just like you, I see,' said Soutine with a laugh.

'Mama? Oh, no, sometimes she loves to talk and tell stories, and they're so funny that we both laugh till we cry, and practically fall down, we laugh so much. And sometimes she tells me such frightening stories that I can't go to sleep afterwards! Well, now, where am I to throw all this rubbish? There's a whole mountain of it!' Marika had swept all the rubbish into a corner of the studio.

'Very good, very good, thank you. I'll get a sheet, dump everything into it and put it in the bathroom.'

'The bathroom? How are you going to wash then?' cried my daughter in surprise, and stood there with her arms at her sides, gazing round-eyed at Soutine.

'That's all right, I go to the public baths anyway, in the rue de la Gaieté. I'm afraid of lighting the gas myself, ever since an accident I had once.'

'Oh, very well,' conceded Marika, 'you throw the rubbish into the bathroom, and I'll put the kettle on for tea. I'm parched with all that dust.'

'What a daughter to have, Marevna! A regular firebrand!'

'And bossy too,' I added.

'Oh, I know you painters—all you want is people to sit still and pose for you, without stirring a finger!' grumbled Marika, biting into her bread.

'Why does she talk only French and no Russian?' asked Soutine.

'It's because she goes to a French school, and says she has to speak French well, otherwise they all tease her and call her "the Russian" or "the Russian Mexican". There's nothing to be done with her!'

'Yes, that's the sort of daughter I'd like to have myself,' said Soutine.

I asked Soutine whether he had ever married and whether he had any children.

'Oh, no, I'm not married, and I don't intend to be. I was wedded to my art long ago. And as for children, Dr Faure, who has been treating me for a long time now, says I can't have any. I don't know whether to be glad or sorry. We Jews love our families and children, but you know, a family often prevents a painter, or any artist, from working seriously, though of course there are exceptions. An artist often has to compromise and sell bad work for the market, for the art-mongers, to be able to feed his family. And the result is a real decline in creative art. Oh, it isn't a bad thing to have a family, if you don't exaggerate things, like my parents, who had eleven children, or Modi's, who had thirteen—and Chagall, too, had eleven brothers and sisters! It's hard to feed such big families, and they're usually half-starved. It would be better for the rich to have lots of children, but it's usually the poor who do. Why is that?' Soutine's expression changed as he spoke: at one moment he was smiling and the next had lapsed suddenly into gloom.

Soutine came to see us at the rue des Créts, where I had a large studio with a room upstairs, a balcony and two terraces. He had lunch and drank tea, and then he asked to look at my work. He liked a portrait of Marika, a landscape and a still-life, all painted in the pointillist style, I thought that Soutine could not possibly admire my paintings, but he said, 'Believe me, I really do like them. Of course, pointillism is not new, but you use it so individually—I've never seen a style like it. These are really good. They remind me of frescoes or of woven tapestries. I remember one cubist picture of yours that Saugrade bought—and Zborowski wanted to buy it from him. I never touched Cubism myself, you know, although I was attracted by it at one time. When I was painting at Céret and at Cagnes I yielded to its influence in spite of myself, and the results were not entirely banal. But then, Marevna, Céret itself is anything but banal. There is so much foreshortening in the landscape that, for that very reason, a picture may seem to have been painted in some specific style. Anyway, it's only interesting to paint landscapes as you want to, as you see them, not as you're supposed to see them. After all, every painter has his own "temperament", his own point of view, his own imagery—don't forget this is most important of all—even in painting landscapes; and that's why each painter's creative work is different. Admittedly, it was easy to become involved with cubism, and indeed it could even give one a lot. But to stay with it too long and take it as a goal for the attainment of "the highest point in art"—that I find inadmissible.'

I remembered that Rivera had said almost exactly the same thing before his departure for Mexico in 1921.

'Marevna, you must do what you want to do, what can further enrich you. You must be free in your creative work—that is the most important thing, I'm sure of it!' said Soutine thoughtfully.

I also showed him my weaving and my models for a *maison de couture*, with which I was regularly earning enough to live on. He was delighted, and said enthusiastically to Marika, 'You have a Mama with golden hands!'

At this Marika could no longer keep silent. 'You know, Soutine, sometimes when Mama is ill—and in winter that's all the time— it's I who take her pictures to sell to Zamaron at the Préfecture. There are lots of policemen there. And sometimes I sell my own work. I sign it "Marika Rivera".'

Soutine formed the habit of visiting us. One day we had finished lunch and were drinking our coffee, when he jumped up suddenly as if he had been stung, dashed to the balcony and looked down. 'My goodness,' he cried, I'd quite forgotten that Petrov stayed in the taxi. He must have gone to sleep. Excuse me and thank you for lunch. I must go and look after him!'

I remembered Petrov, a tall, fair, handsome young man, very pale and rumpled looking, said to be talented, but an inveterate drunkard and in very poor health. Later he married an Englishwoman in Nice and died not long afterwards. 'Why didn't you bring him in?' I asked.

'Oh, he's still drunk from last night's drinking session. He slept at my place and hasn't come round yet.' And Soutine dashed off down the stairs.

'That Soutine!' said Marika, looking out into the street, 'He leaves his friend in the taxi like an umbrella, and the poor fellow was waiting for him all the time. How much will the taxi cost him, Mama?'

When Soutine asked Marika to sit to him, she said, 'D'you know, it's an awful misery for me, posing. It's very hard to pose for Mama. Oh, what fierce eyes she makes when she's working, and if I get up, why, sometimes she throws books at me! "Sit down", she says. I bet you aren't like that. You don't do things like that, do you?'

'Who, me?' laughed Soutine. 'Why, I sometimes throw the picture, a chair, a table or my easel to the floor, and fall down myself, yelling blue murder.'

Marika opened her eyes wide in surprise. 'Oh, well, then I'll never pose for you, if you're like that. You scare me.' Indeed, when Soutine asked her seriously two or three more times to sit for him she refused categorically. 'No, no, you'd better paint Mama, Soutine, and I'll just watch,' she would say.

Soutine told me he preferred painting landscapes to painting portraits. 'To do a portrait, it's necessary to take one's time, but the model tires quickly and assumes a stupid expression. Then it's necessary to hurry up and that irritates me. I become unnerved. I grind my teeth, and sometimes it gets to a point where I scream, I slash the canvas, and everything goes to hell, and I fall down on the floor. I always implore them to pose without saying a word and without stirring their arms and legs. Once the models understand that they are helping me work by sitting still and saying nothing, all goes well. But you see, this is the way I'm made. Sometimes the model is all right, but then something goes wrong with the work. I lose my outline of the nose, the mouth or the eyes, or something else, and things are going wrong—I suddenly see flames before me and feel them burning me. I begin to scream and throw everything on the floor. I admit that this is stupid, and even horrible, and I am always terrified at this moment, but afterwards, like a woman in childbirth, I'm exhausted but certain that the picture will be better. Why is this, I wonder?'

I think a doctor could have given him an answer. Perhaps those were epileptic fits without which Soutine could not create: it was as though his art was indissolubly bound to his disease.

I also think that Soutine increased his difficulties by deliberately or unconsciously ignoring drawing in his works, especially his portraits, which he outlined directly in paint. Once, showing Soutine some drawings of Modi's which I had kept—a portrait of Rivera with a pipe, two portraits of me and several heads from the Rotonde—I asked Soutine to do a sketch of me as a memento. I had never seen a drawing of his.

Soutine sat down at the table, took a sheet of paper, got a pencil out of a box, screwed up his eyes, puffed up his lips and began to look at me as if I had turned into a turkey. He stared at me for some time, then started doing something on the paper. 'You know, Marevna, I could do an interesting portrait of you in oils. It's a pity we didn't think of it before, because I have to go to the country, but we'll simply postpone it until the autumn. In oils, now, my portraits come out; they even say that the likenesses are good. As for the drawing—no, it's no good, I can't give it to you. I haven't enough patience to draw. When I was at school in Minsk they made us draw, of course, and the teachers would scold me for not drawing like the other pupils. I could do it, I assure you, but not in the way they wanted and not like the others. And when we had to make charcoal drawings of some Apollo or Venus or Minerva—I had a wonderful time! My goodness, I used to draw gods for them! They were all like the old bodies I used to know in Smilovichi!' And Soutine would smile at these youthful reminiscences.

He tore the drawing into small pieces, and never painted my portrait.

* * *

Time passed quickly when we met. Soutine liked to talk about his childhood and youth, about his work and hopes, about artists and other people. I could feel in him the loneliness of a lost soul.

He was peaceable and quiet; he liked anecdotes and laughter. But sometimes he would suddenly flare up, scream irritably, flush scarlet and then grow pale; his left eye would begin to revolve rapidly in its orbit and white foam would gather at the corners of his mouth. All this would mark the beginning of an attack, and he would become terrible to behold—like Frankenstein's monster!

Soutine could not bear to be alone, and always had by him a friend with whom to drink, to argue about art and painters, to share everything—not least to serve as a patient nurse for him at times. One evening, as we came back from the cinema, he asked me to stay the night with him, and I did. He was a poor lover, perhaps because of shyness. What he thirsted for above all was tenderness and affection.

Looking through some books on Soutine's shelves one day, I was surprised to see one entitled *L'homme du monde* ('The man of the world'), containing instructions on how to behave in polite society. Of course, I had heard rumours that Soutine had been changed by his increasing wealth, that he had several apartments with bathrooms, that he had a private chauffeur, that he wore a black silk dinner jacket in the evenings and that generally he had become a bourgeois. I had thought how given the public is to flights of fancy and exaggeration when talking about artists.

Opening the book at random, I read, 'You must clean your teeth in the morning and evening and after meals. This is necessary to keep your breath sweet. There is nothing more reprehensible in society than bad breath. After a meal, take a toothpick and, hiding your mouth with a napkin, clean out the particles of food from between your teeth. At table, you must *never* pick your teeth with a match, a pin or your fork.' I burst out laughing.

'You know, Marevna, it was Oscar Meshchaninov who gave me this book when he no longer needed it. His father was a tailor, like mine, and wanted to make his son a tailor, just as mine did, but Oscar became an excellent sculptor. When I came to Paris in 1913, Oscar used to teach me what and what not to do, and he often told me in those early days, "Chaim, don't pick your teeth with your fork."'

This amused me too, for when I had first met Oscar, he himself had had that habit, but I refrained from mentioning this to Soutine.

'Everyone who sees this book on my shelf laughs like mad. "Soutine, you want to be a man of the world, with that face? Oh, that's a joke, devilishly funny, but really, you know, give up the idea!" And that dinner jacket too—it doesn't go with my Kalmuk face. I've often heard people say, "You see that man with a face like a monkey? He's a Russian Jew, a madman, and his pictures are crazy too, but he makes good money, and they say that when he dies his pictures will be worth two or three times more than they are now." So everybody buys them. Now I've become educated. I've learned to speak French and I'm reading Bergson's philosophy, though I must admit it's hard to understand. But at my age, you know, it's difficult to learn good manners. Sometimes I feel an urge to belch at table (and with my digestion this often happens), sometimes to use a fork to pick my teeth. It's a very handy way, you know, but people say, "Oh, how vulgar!" At home in Smilovichi, we all operated with our forks at table.' And Soutine laughed heartily.

A long time afterwards, in 1962, I was reminded of this conversation when I saw Ossip Zadkine on a London television programme. Zadkine said, 'Many years ago, my father sent me to London to learn English, to finish my education and, mainly, to learn good manners, to become a gentleman. Well, I finished my education and learned to speak English, but as for good manners —no, that was difficult. I hadn't too much time for that, but I didn't play cricket too badly.' And Zadkine burst out laughing. I am sure that such simple frankness before an audience of 6,000,000 people could only have aroused sympathy and liking for him—after all, he had learned to play the game which the English esteem on a level with Shakespeare!

Soutine told me once, with a broad grin, 'You know, Marevna, when I first came to Paris, I was still so naïve and simple that people—even my closest friends—used to laugh at me and tell all kinds of anecdotes about me. Having devoted all my time to painting and visiting museums, I knew little about life and women, and I had little money to spend on them—I could only afford cheap prostitutes and *petites femmes* from the cafés. It was easy to make a fool of me, to deceive me, to have a good laugh at my expense.'

I recalled the stories Soutine's friends of those days used to tell about him. For example, one day he had the unexpected luck to pick up a young girl who was ready and willing, but he did not know how to receive her.

'*Primo*,' his friends said, 'buy a toothbrush. Next, buy a clean shirt and last, put a sheet on your bed. Like that it should go off all right.'

So Soutine did as instructed. The girl came and very quickly made off again, never to return. Soutine was very disheartened.

'What went wrong?' his friends asked. 'How did you set about it?'

'I bought a toothbrush, as you told me, and put it in a glass. I also bought a shirt, which cost me a great deal, and spread it out on a chair, so that she could see it properly. Then I turned the sheet on my bed over. But obviously she was a high-class tart— she didn't want to go to bed with one sheet.'

Now, of course, things were different. When Soutine's fame as a talented painter began to spread and the prices of his pictures to rise, rich patrons, well-known collectors and owners of large galleries began to ask him to smart dinners, receptions and gala evenings. Soutine was not overwhelmed. 'People think and say that Europeans and rich people have good manners, that they are "cultivated", but I say nothing of the sort! "Good manners" are relative, and very often they are only superficial. You know, when I start cleaning up my studio for a guest, I'm apt to brush up the mess (not like they do in the streets) and sweep it under the rug to hide it, and I think that everything is all right. But the rubbish gradually finds its way out from under the carpet. It's the same with people. They pretend to be well brought up and to have good manners, but every now and then the rubbish—the bad manners —rises to the surface.'

From my own experience of the world, I found it perfectly

natural that Soutine's popularity should grow with his renown; also, that the ladies should start to flutter round him 'like moths round a flame,' he told me. But his attitude toward society ladies was one of scepticism and mistrust. 'If I spent all my time with them, I'd soon be unable to paint a single good picture. That's why I go away from Paris so often, although I love it. I stifle in the company of ladies, Marevna. Now they've dreamed me into a silk dinner jacket and think they can lead me around like a dancing bear, a new clown! And these society ladies, excuse me, like to play around and even to behave like street-walkers. Things have changed now. "Freedom" is the cry. They say that this behaviour is chic, dashing. These polite society ladies are just like lapdogs. They are sick to death of their pretence of good manners, and they think that with Soutine they can let themselves go. For them, I'm a lout and a savage, for in many ways I've remained as I was.

'Some coquette decides that she wants a picture of mine free (oh, she'll tell her husband that Soutine gave it to her!) and begins to try to turn my head—thinking that there could be no brains in such a simple head as mine! She comes driven by a chauffeur in a smart limousine, all in silk and lace or practically naked under her fur coat, to make an effect, to seduce the simpleton! She'll be smelling like a scent shop, and altogether everything is done for chic, brilliance, elegance. But by now I've become wise—I'm either ill, away or busy—and the lady goes away furious! Perhaps she's already told her friends that that fool Soutine had given her a picture, or perhaps she's already found a good purchaser. You know, I've become so wise in the ways of the world that I'm surprised at myself.

'Eventually I give in to the lady. Why waste time making enemies? And there's nothing more poisonous than an enraged female! Once I wanted to give a little lady a still-life of a chicken as a souvenir. It was a good still-life, but she looked at it and asked, "Isn't there anything else?" I said there wasn't, which happened to be true. The lady took offence and flounced out without saying goodbye. I remember that at home "chicken" was a term of abuse—"Oh, you brainless chicken!" we used to say. And

I remembered, too, how my father used to call me "chicken" when I could not understand a problem in algebra, and how offended I would get.

'Well, then, I showed this still-life to an admirer of my work, of my "morbid" still-lifes, and he gave me the price I asked straight away. The "Chicken" is now in America, and the buyer was—the lady's husband. She tried to do me down, but it turned out the other way round! No, Marevna, I know you're always defending women, but men are really much better. Of course, some men too are terrible swindlers, but still they respect me, although I don't belong to their society. I simply represent capital to them. They speculate on my pictures and don't bother to conceal it. And then, some of them like my work, as they like Russian salad or pickled herrings. "Morbid!" they say, snapping their fingers, and are even very friendly to me sometimes.'

There was much naïve cynicism, irony and some bitterness in Soutine's judgments. Of course, he could not be a ladies' man, for he was neither a dancer, a sportsman, a dandy nor any of the things which make men attractive to women. Apart from being ugly, he did not invent compliments for ladies nor did he flatter them; on the contrary, he distorted their beauty when painting their portraits (not out of malice but because in his art there was no need for the beauty they could offer) and this women find hard to accept. But when they heard him called 'a painter of genius,' they were none the less flattered. Then, too, some women simply have a weakness for 'geniuses'. Personally, I was sorry for Soutine, being sure that not a single one of his lady admirers was worthy of him.

I remember vividly the time Soutine came to me for advice. 'I'm in a very difficult position,' he told me. 'My father has somehow found out that I'm earning good money now, that I'm rich, and he's written inviting me to go out there and help him—his house is falling down, the boat's no good any more, there are no boots, he's ill, and lots, lots more. Here, read it for yourself.' He handed me a letter closely written in Russian. 'What am I to do, eh?'

'Do you or don't you feel drawn to see your family?' I asked.

'Well, of course, he writes that it'll only be for a visit, but on the other hand one must be careful. If I decide to go, they'll certainly let me in. Why not? I've done no harm to anyone. But will they let me out to come back here? I've got my work all laid out here, you know. Though I've had very hard times, now I can earn as much as I want to. But over there, who knows what awaits me and my painting? Even here, I practically starved at first. No one would buy my pictures—they frightened people. And what if my father starts to curse me again, to call me a slobberer? What if with him I go back to being a wretched, good-for-nothing, sick boy?'

'But think, your parents are old now!'

'Yes, my mother is already dead,' said Soutine gloomily, squinting at some point in space far beyond my head. 'There's only my father left, and he'll die soon too.'

'But don't you want to see your homeland, those fields and forests you love and miss so much? Perhaps when you see your own country again you'll be rejuvenated and you'll begin to paint even better.'

'These are all just words, Marevna. After all, we don't know how they're living there, how the Jews are treated.'

'But you can see for yourself that your old father isn't dead yet. He survived the great change. Your mother may have died of exhaustion, fatigue, malnutrition, but now they're changing everything. There are more people everywhere. Life is gayer. Forget the past! Forgive the old man!'

'Oh, yes, my father writes that too. "Forgive that I used to beat you," he says. "It was good for you. Now you've become a gentleman. Don't throw your money about, save it." That's my father, always a miser. We were always hungry. I'm sure my mother died of starvation—she gave everything to him and to the children—and now the old man comes whining, "Don't waste money, save it!" This letter has depressed me, Marevna, really it has. Although he's my father, he seems like a stranger. He never loved me, believe me, and now he writes for help! I'll send him some money, and let him do what he likes. It won't bring my mother back to life. But I won't go there—no, he was too unjust to me.'

What could I say to Soutine, when he was obviously unable to forget his sad childhood? I was touched by his avowals and by his confidence in me, and I felt compassion for his pessimism and his cynicism.

* * *

Soutine's devotion to art, his serious and honest approach to his work and its execution were extremely attractive in their sincerity. He often mercilessly destroyed his less successful works, painted during his early years in Paris. On one occasion, at the Salle Drouot, he saw a picture of his which was being sold among others from a collection, bought it and tore it to pieces before the eyes of the amazed and indignant spectators. 'Absolute muck!' he announced. His intolerance of any compromise in regard to his work inspired both astonishment and respect.

At the rue St Gothard in Cagnes, Soutine emulated Rembrandt in painting some interesting pictures of butcher's meat, with results so real and forceful as to seem hardly credible. In his 'Carcass of an Ox', the carcass is split in half and hung up by the hind legs against a blue and green background; it forms a triangle. The legs, with the feet cut off, of course, and the whole carcass resemble a human torso hung up by the thighs, without feet or hands but with a shapeless, crushed little head. The colours of the meat are splendid, but the general impression is somehow unhealthy. While he was working, the flesh he was painting began to spoil and its colour to darken, and Soutine obtained from the butcher fresh blood, which he poured over the rotting meat. It was summertime, and the meat began to reek. Enormous green flies swarmed round the door of Soutine's ground-floor studio like bees round a hive: dismayed neighbours and passers-by complained to the police. Soutine made his explanations, cursing in Russian, asking the gendarmes to leave him in peace to finish his work, spraying them with saliva, stamping his feet, almost weeping. But he was obliged to give up the rotting carcass. By then he

166

Soutine: **Carcass of an ox**
Reconstruction **by Marevna** (see fig. 11)

was himself permeated from head to foot with its revolting smell. People shied away from him, and children pointed at him and jeered, 'There goes the carrion-eater!' But what was all that beside the wonderful painting planned so long before and so successfully realized?

Soutine admired Rembrandt not only as a supreme master and great humanist, but also because he was absorbed in Jews and their art and depicted many incidents from Jewish life. In 1931, when Soutine was staying with his friend and patron M. Castaing at Lèves in the Eure-et-Loire, he decided to fulfil a cherished ambition to paint a 'woman bathing' after Rembrandt. The river was there, and there were peasant women about, but none of them wanted to pose. At last, for a monetary consideration offered by M. Castaing, one woman agreed to pose standing in the water in her night shirt. The site was chosen. Soutine was radiant. The easel and canvas were brought, the palette and brushes were ready, but the peasant woman suddenly refused to raise her skirt and show her legs up to the knee. Soutine implored her to raise it just a little, if only to make the gesture. At last she agreed, reluctantly, and he began to paint furiously.

Meanwhile, heavy clouds had gathered. A storm was drawing near. When the first claps of thunder sounded, the woman prepared to flee, but Soutine managed to persuade her to stay. Then the rain started. The woman climbed out of the water and began to run. Soutine pursued her and caught up with her. There they stood under the pouring rain, struggling and vociferating—she calling on God and all the saints (not people, no, that would have been too humiliating!) to save her from this madman, and he yelling at her not to run away but to go back and pose. The struggle ended with both of them falling into the water.

Soutine managed to finish the picture on another occasion, and it is regarded as one of the best paintings of that period. There is no beauty in the peasant woman, only realism. The picture is constructed on the basis of a triangle and a sphere.

In 1934, in the same village, Soutine wanted to paint again a subject he had already depicted in 1917, a 'woman lying on the

Soutine: Woman bathing
Reconstruction by Marevna (see fig. 13)

grass' under a tree, after Courbet's 'Mademoiselle près de la rivière'. Soutine was strongly attracted to the nineteenth-century master, both as a painter and as a strong-willed, progressive friend of the people, who had once declared that he was not only a socialist, but a democrat and a republican, that he was an advocate of any revolution and that he would raise not only the banner of revolution but also the banner of art, of the realism which he believed to be essential for mankind.

Soutine persuaded the estate agent's wife to pose for him lying on the grass, but when the lady's husband learned of this and saw the unfinished canvas, he was furious and forbade his wife to pose any more. Soutine was desperate. He cursed the husband and begged to be allowed to finish the picture. Then the landlord, seeing the artist in an almost hysterical condition and appreciating the work in progress, came to Soutine's aid and persuaded the agent not to prevent his wife from posing. The agent reluctantly gave his consent grinding his teeth.

Sometimes the paints Soutine used were not of the best quality and deteriorated on the canvas after they were mixed; the thick layers of paint he liked to use cracked after drying (especially the dark blues, reds and blacks), spoiling the whole aspect of the picture. In 1928, in my presence, Soutine telephoned a client and asked him how the red dress in the portrait of his wife was faring, and received the reply that the red dress had unfortunately cracked in several places. 'Well, my friend, please send me back the picture, since it's imperfect, and I'll return your cheque for twenty thousand francs. I'd be very grateful if you would do this quickly. No, no, sir, I cannot do otherwise.'

The client was reluctant to return the picture and assured Soutine that the cracked paint did not look at all bad. This agitated the painter. He grew red as beet and began to stammer and shout into the receiver, showering it with saliva. 'If an artist returns your money, you are obliged to send him back his spoiled picture. You must! It is dishonest to keep it. A flaw in the paint spoils a picture and the reputation of the artist, don't you understand?'

When the conversation terminated, unsuccessfully, Soutine was trembling. 'The scoundrel!' he shouted. 'I suppose he's afraid that when I've repaired the picture I'll ask twice as much for it or that I won't let him have it back or that I'll tear it up! That would probably be best. I'd have to scrape off the whole dress. Colours in Paris are quite worthless, the devil take them!' His left eye began to swivel round and his face grew deathly pale, a tremor seizing his cheeks and his foaming mouth.

I went to the kitchen to get him some water and put the glass in front of him. The crisis passed, and the eye of 'Frankenstein's monster' stopped swivelling.

'Please forgive me, I am not myself.' He swallowed the water greedily. 'Please, I beg you, let's go away from here, somewhere else, to a café. I'm upset, somehow.'

We went to a café near the Gare Montparnasse, where there were lots of people, but none of those who frequented the Rotonde and the Dôme. Watching the crowds, we reminisced about the war years, when that café had been full of soldiers and *petites femmes légères* and when we had sometimes gone to the station to watch Ehrenburg hauling sacks and crates to earn a few francs—a sight which aroused both our pity and our admiration for the poet.

* * *

Death is always terrible, but some forms of it are even more terrible because they are tragic. Some deaths are like a last chord, an organ finale, and by putting an end to a human being's existence, they show us the full meaning of that life. I consider that Soutine's death was no less tragic than that of Max Jacob.

In 1941–1943, during the last war, Soutine lived at Champigny-sur-Veuldre with his friends and patrons the Castaings and went on working, though more slowly and less prolifically than before. I think that he no longer hurried with his work because he realized that there was no reason to hurry; and such late works as his 'Mother and Child' show that his painting was even more inspired. Early on in the war, like many other artists, he was invited by some Americans to spend the duration in the United States, but he refused categorically, preferring to remain in France. Strange as it may seem, he was not subjected to persecution by the Germans; perhaps they let him alone because he was an emigrant, or perhaps the 'morbidity' of his work appealed to them. Generally speaking, he had withdrawn from life. Friends and colleagues, including Kikoine and Kremègne, the companions of his youth, now had families, but Soutine remained single, devoting his life to his ruling passion—his art. He was not a chaste recluse, for he had liaisons with a number of women, who sat for him and sometimes nursed him. He continued to suffer, as he had suffered all his life, from fits and stomach ulcers.

In August of 1943 he suffered a very serious attack and was rushed to Paris for an operation. According to his friend, the painter Grimm, Soutine was unable to endure the drive, jolting over two hundred kilometres. Though he was still alive when he reached Dr Olivier's clinic, where the great surgeon Gausset performed the operation, Soutine died on the table. He was not yet fifty.

Soutine was a vagabond, unable to stay in one place long without becoming nervous and querulous. Throughout his life in France, which he loved sincerely as his second country, Soutine was fully and painfully aware that he was an emigrant and a Jew. Like the wandering Jew he travelled all over the country, seeking inspiration for his creative vein. Inevitably he returned to Paris, which he loved, though here too he constantly changed apartments, perhaps to avoid importunate people wanting help or pictures and inquisitive journalists. And so it was in 1943 that he returned to Paris, this time forever. He was laid to rest in the Montparnasse Cemetery, where his friend Modigliani is also buried.

* * *

Aesthetics is the science of theoretical analysis, it enables one to see an artist's creative capacity, the structure of his works, his outlook, his ideas, his subject matter, his aesthetic ideals and his innermost soul in greater depth. That is why it is essential to maintain a close connection between the artist and aesthetics.

A critical analysis of the science of aesthetics shows that it also comprises certain separate elements of works of art; these are beauty and ugliness, tragedy and caricature. For instance, in Soutine's creative work, it may be said that the tragic and comic elements undoubtedly predominate. The structural and colour images of the artist's creation are an aesthetic reflection of the life around him; Soutine's childhood and youth implanted in his soul a tragi-comic view of his environment and of the people he met.

The reader will no doubt have noticed that one of the main reasons for my great admiration of Soutine's work is his interest in and devotion to structure. I should, therefore, like to explain and illustrate with diagrams the construction of some of his paintings and indicate the masters who influenced him most. I must preface these explanations with some general reflections on the aesthetics of structure in art.

In the medieval art of the Italian primitives and in Renaissance painting, which often took the form of frescoes on the walls of churches and vast castle halls, a knowledge of perspective and foreshortening was essential for depicting landscapes and figures on panels placed at some distance and at an angle from the viewer's eye.

All visible objects have three dimensions—length, breadth and height. The relationship between objects has to be conveyed by combining them in simple geometric figures: pyramids, prisms, cubes and cones, according to the precepts of Giotto, Leonardo and Cézanne. That is why the theory of construction by means of perspective and foreshortening begins with the study of the laws of depiction by *straight, parallel* and *diagonal lines, squares, cubes* and *pyramids*. These can encompass any composition, by the emergence from the intersection of vertical, horizontal and diagonal lines of the triangles and angles which are indispensable for the full harmony of the structure of a picture. Then come the colours, which also play a vital part in the ultimate product. But to achieve general harmony, movement is essential. Giotto and

Leonardo da Vinci attained the remarkable harmony of their frescoes and paintings by always including in them one or two circles.

The simplest method of constructing a painting is to transpose the length of the *shorter side* of the rectangle formed by the canvas to the *longer side*. By repeating this operation on the other side of the rectangle, two new rectangles with two new centres are obtained; these two new planes have equal dimensions and can enter into one another. The artist then draws diagonal lines across each of the *three rectangles*, which are thus interwoven and form a grid, like embroidery canvas, on which natural, original forms (objects, people and landscapes) fall into shapes lent to them by the design of the grid.

But there is yet another way of dividing planes, which is more complex and attracts experienced and inquisitive minds. Leonardo da Vinci called this method 'the divine proportion'. It was asserted that the law of organic growth is in some cases based on the Golden Number which mathematicians use in certain equations, which is extremely interesting for experts and which Vitruvius described as follows: 'To make something which is divided into unequal parts seem beautiful, the ratio between the smaller and the larger parts must be the same as the ratio between the larger part and the whole'.

All Renaissance paintings were constructed on this principle, and it may also be discerned in some Pompeian frescoes. It is interesting to note that the same principle may be found in Byzantine icons; this method of plane construction was probably introduced from Greece and Byzantium into Italy, where it was adopted by the medieval painters. In France, after the Gothic painters, Poussin was practically the only major artist to follow the principle until Courbet and Seurat in the nineteenth century, succeeded by Cézanne and his cubist followers such as Cerusier, Juan Gris, Picasso, Rivera. Although Cubism did not remain fashionable for long and soon died out, interesting and valid reflections of it may still be found in certain paintings.

* * *

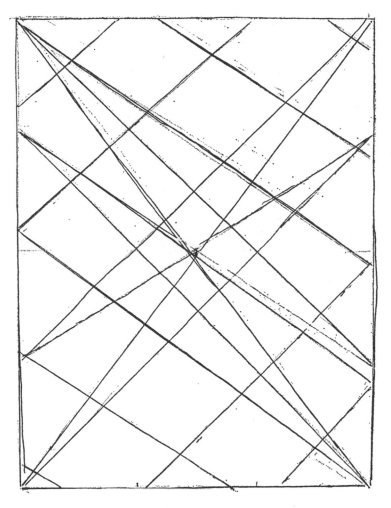

Diagram of simple composition

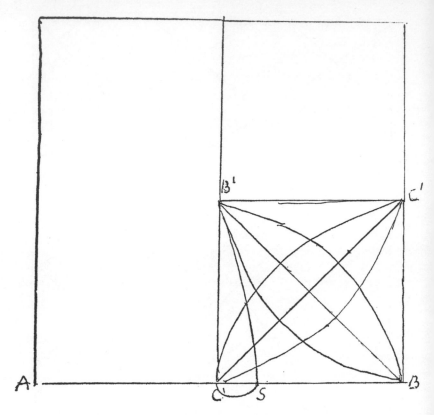

Diagram of the Golden Section

In 1918 Renoir is reported to have said, 'Young painters nowadays want to be "artists" before they have mastered their very
difficult art. They say that life is too short to become a "master"
and they will be content with what they can learn at the rue
Bonaparte [the Paris school of Fine Arts]—just like obtaining a
driving licence!' This criticism cannot apply to Soutine—that
'true follower of Cézanne', according to Rivera. Truly dedicated
students of painting seek out and discover the mysteries and
secrets of art in the works of the Old Masters, which show them

176

why their own work has been misunderstood and why they have been not only neglected, but even persecuted at various times in their lives. It has been said that one must have great talent to make one's genius understood; I think that this is absolutely true and that Soutine was a really creative artist because he worked unremittingly in his search for the essence of art and the essence of its mastery. Like Cézanne, he would wander about the Louvre and would stand for hours in front of a picture by one of his favourite masters, trying to find in it something mysterious and profound, concealed from profane and inexperienced eyes. And he seems to have found it: one can now stand for hours in front of one of Soutine's pictures and see and feel everything that lives in it and all that Soutine wants to convey to us, sometimes with a quiet smile and sometimes shouting and foaming at the mouth.

Like his friends, Kremègne and Kikoine, Soutine was greatly influenced by the expressionists, whose work he first came to know as a student at Vilna. The expressionist movement began in Germany at the beginning of the century. It was principally characterized by a critical attitude towards bourgeois society and culture and by protest against the general indifference to the terrible living conditions of workers and peasants. Through their works, the expressionist painters accused society of egoism and indifference to art; they sought to eliminate exploitation and to achieve absolute freedom. In the vanguard of expressionist art were Hödler, Münch, Ensor and Van Gogh, and in 1905 a group of these artists met at Dresden to found a movement called '*Die Brücke*', subsequently exhibiting many portraits of people distorted and deformed by their hard, abnormal lives.

Soutine was greatly struck by this art of distortion; the deformed world of his own childhood was strangely similar to the one depicted by the expressionist painters. For some time he was influenced by Ensor, Münch, Kokoschka, and especially by Van Gogh. The personality of the Dutch painter—that Don Quixote figure, as he is often called—stands out sharply among those of other artists and undoubtedly held a great attraction for Soutine. Van Gogh's life as an artist and as a man was a stark tragedy because of his character and because of his art: the puritanical bourgeois society of his time was completely indifferent to the life of the poor, to the peasants and to this talented painter who came from a poor family and who tragically portrayed the miserable lives of the working people and the realistic side of the world around him. One of the young Dutchman's earliest paintings is of a poor family eating a wretched supper of potatoes round a table in a dimly-lit kitchen; and the attitudes and hungry faces of the workers and their children gathered round the steaming dish are marvellously touching. The picture is painted boldly, in dark colours, with thick brush strokes; its great value lies in the fact that it is the first example of the young artist's creative realism. Loneliness, poverty and the struggle for his ideals and artistic expression gradually sapped the painter's energy, and in a moment of despair he killed himself. Predictably, it was only after his death that society and the public at large realized his immense significance as a man and as an artist.

On arriving in Paris in 1913, Soutine was soon caught up in the great chaotic maelstrom of the 'New Art', for in addition to Expressionism and Fauvism, there was Cubism, which had begun to emerge in 1905–1906. All the young artists of the time fought the battle of 'New Art' in the arena of Cubism; Soutine was naturally as interested in this new 'ism' as anyone else, and sought from Diego Rivera an explanation of its meaning and essence. Rivera had made a profound study of the structure of painting, and it was he who opened Soutine's eyes to the manner in which that structure had evolved from the geometrical influence of astrology on architecture, through the Pompeian frescoes, the trecento painters, Giotto, Leonardo da Vinci, Poussin, Courbet, culminating finally in Cézanne, the real originator of Cubism; the outcome of his desire to transform Impressionism into something more solid and constructive.

In the work of the generation of painters who emerged after the overthrow of the Second Empire and the establishment of the Second Republic, the 'subject' lost its importance and paramount significance was attached to 'light effects' and to the inter-

178

relationships of colour tones in nature. The appellation 'Impressionism' was fully justified, for it pointed to the essential difference between the New Art and Realism. For the first time, artists began to paint out of doors, and in casting Realism aside they admitted only one element of reality, *light*, in depicting nature. The early works of such impressionists as Monet, Pissaro and Sisley retain some elements of natural life, but as time went on practically all the objects and nature itself became diffused in a stream of light, turning everything into a dazzling kaleidoscope. As Jean Cocteau wrote, 'Impressionism has let off its fireworks to mark the end of a long festival, and now the time has come for a new form of art'.

Cézanne alone stood apart from the impressionists, having no faith in the permanence of this art form and no belief in the representation of nature as a mirage. He began to construct on his canvases a new world, based on rules and doctrines created by himself. He had seriously studied the Italian primitives and Giotto, as well as the works of the Italian Renaissance painters, Tintoretto and Titian, Rembrandt and Courbet, whom he admired particularly (as Soutine did after him).

For Cézanne, colour was from the outset only a secondary problem. According to him, 'When the form attains its own perfection, then the colour also assumes its own richness'. He did not paint pretty, bourgeois still-lifes, but constantly sought structural planes, depth and volume. His landscapes and portraits were painted with the same end in view, for he believed that a face, a tree, a house or a bottle each present the same problem to the artist and must be portrayed according to the same rules. His structure is that of an architect; his execution that of a mosaic artist, for his brush strokes resemble those of the pointillists.

Planes, volume, form and colour are what we see in Cézanne's pictures, no sentimentality, no romanticism. And yet his Provençal landscapes and portraits—indeed, all his portraits of peasants— are imbued with transcendent poetry. He loved his Provence above all else; according to him, it helped him to develop his creative capacity. 'His art is a mass of force and harmony, to which nothing can be added and from which nothing can be subtracted,'

Reconstructions of Giotto's fresco and Courbet's little girl and bird

Dr Faure wrote of Cézanne.

When I was in Amsterdam in 1929, I visited a Cézanne-Van Gogh exhibition where you could pass from the French painter's room to that of the Dutchman, and it was amazing that the works of these two very different artists did not jar, but complemented one another. Cézanne impresses us by his architectural structure and the harmony of his forms, rather than by his colours, whereas Van Gogh strikes us by the strength of his imagination and by his colourful, brilliant landscapes and portraits from Provence— practically the same subjects as Cézanne's. For Cézanne, the subject was simply a pretext for finding a successful composition, whereas Van Gogh let his imagination run riot, and his portraits are full of deep spirituality, as well as character. Rivera was convinced that Soutine's paintings would eventually bear comparison with Cézanne's because he was able to combine Cézanne's architectural structure with Van Gogh's deep inner feeling.

Cézanne's contribution to art is so great and significant that he can surely be forgiven for his abstraction and his isolation from the world of mankind. After all, an artist's life is relatively short, taking into account that most artists are poor and that years of near starvation, illness, study and work take their toll of strength and energy. Fortunately Cézanne was spared much of the struggle because his father left him a small income; he lived modestly with his wife and son and an old gardener. All three of them posed for him, the gardener often posing in the nude, even representing women bathers: such considerations as sex were of no interest to an artist, who was concerned only with movement, form and composition. He gave his whole life to this search and only a short time before his death said ruefully, 'Now I could really begin to paint properly.' He died like a warrior on the battlefield, of pneumonia contracted while painting a landscape in bad weather.

What Cézanne failed to accomplish during his lifetime was completed by his pupils, who interpreted his teaching and his rules for 'incorporating living forms in a geometrical framework' according to their own lights; the painters of the new Western school declared their main goal to be 'the creation of new abstract plastic forms', and this led to the birth of Cubism.

When the first cubist pictures appeared at the 1905 Salon ('Building bricks or something!' said Matisse about Braque's landscapes), the theory of the new geometrical mysticism was that everything living is illusory and that life itself is a distortion of form. Giotto in the fourteenth century and Cézanne in the nineteenth constructed their compositions out of spheres and triangles in a geometrical framework, but not as explicitly as the Cubists did later. After 1908 the trend was towards using right-angles, cubes, straight lines and flat planes, and by 1912–1913 Cubism was characterized by a complete disintegration of the subject, resulting in the kaleidoscope of component parts which became known as Analytical Cubism. Apollinaire at first complained of the inhumanity of Cubism, but later maintained that 'Cubism constructs, while Dadaism destroys'. Indeed, in their desire to achieve ideal proportions, the cubists have given us works which are more cerebral than sensory, and they express metaphysical forms.

'All earlier art,' wrote Gleize and Metzinger, theorists of Cubism, 'was an effort to depict the outside world which the human eye accepts as something real. Impressionism itself proved that an optical illusion is simply an ordinary fallacy. The real world is a world of geometric shapes. They are embraced by the mind, not accepted by the eye alone. What we see is a deviation from pure form. The goal of art is to attain the essence of things beyond their sensory appearance.'

In 1925 Picasso, another theorist of Cubism, announced: 'We know that art is not the truth, that art is a lie. But this lie is an essential basis of our thought, in that it helps us to create an aesthetical point of view.'

Soutine told me with a laugh one day, when we were talking about the 1914–1918 painters, 'You know, Marevna, every cubist used to say that he was the only real cubist. But Diego Rivera went further—he claimed that he alone knew the secret of Cubism, the secret of the fourth dimension! You know, he once showed me a very strange and amusing construction, with mobile planes made of gelatine leaves—perhaps he even made it himself. Diego used to call the contraption "*la chose*", which came out "*la sozhe*" in his Spanish accent. Many of the cubists used to laugh at Rivera behind his back, and as for him, he quarrelled with all of them, especially with Picasso. He used to call Cubism a "passage" or "corridor", maintaining that it was not an aim in art, but only one of the means of approaching it more closely.'

All this I already knew. In 1916 and 1917, under the influence of the African masks which so fascinated the cubists, Rivera painted two portraits of me, both with white masks instead of faces; in one of the portraits I was recognizable only by the fringe on my forehead and in the other by one blue eye and the shape of my fair hair—the rest was all geometry and fantasy.

When, after three years of genuine fascination with Cubism, Rivera abandoned it in favour of a serious study of Cézanne and El Greco, he told Soutine that these two great masters had made him aware of a cubism which they concealed with 'matter'—with natural forms in their landscapes and with folds of clothing or drapery in their portraits and nudes.

* * *

The only Russian painter I can think of who shared Soutine's fascination with structure and who studied Giotto and Cézanne closely from that point of view was Vrubel. In the late nineteenth and early twentieth centuries in Russia, there was a group, distinct from the many formalistic painters, calling themselves *rayon-nistes*, who stipulated that the shape of an object was determined not by the delineation of its contours and the relation between light and shade, but by the intersection of light rays falling on the object and their reflection on its surface. Vrubel asserted that the contours with which painters usually surround objects and forms do not really exist and are merely an optical illusion, deriving from the interaction of various rays falling on the object and reflected at different angles. He maintained that a colour complementary to the basic colour appears at that point. According to him, 'Cobalt and ochre are the divine colours. Between them they account for the widest variety of shades. You can alter the planes of a completed water-colour by covering it with a light wash of cobalt, and the reds will not become purple or the yellows green—they will only be dimmed and will recede into the background.'

The habit of seeking out planes led Vrubel to a then unusual manner of oil painting, reminiscent of mosaic. Here again, as in his water-colours, he was most concerned with the purity of colours. Although he as yet knew nothing of the pointillist technique, Vrubel freely used optical combinations of colours to achieve maximum clarity and purity. A study of ancient mosaics at Kiev, Ravenna, Venice and Tordello must have been the reason why Vrubel's polychromatic planes, at first barely perceptible, became larger and more noticeable at a short distance, and hence closer to the mosaic technique.

When I went to the Tretyakovsky Gallery for the first time, the pictures which struck me at once and riveted my attention were Vrubel's 'Spirit of the Woods' and 'Daemon'. The combination of colours in such chaotic execution amazed and delighted me. When asked whether I had liked the works of Repin or other more esoteric painters, I replied frankly that I had only really admired the Vrubels. Perhaps it was partly because of his wonderful imagery or because of the deep feeling of solitude in the pictures I have mentioned, but most of all it was because of the colours. What colours!

I see a definite affinity between Vrubel's work and Soutine's, but the earlier painter did not have the same gift of bringing everything into chaotic life. After composing the structure of his pictures, Soutine proceeded to make them live. Everything in them seems to move, to whirl about; the trees bend first in one direction and then in another, as in his landscape 'A Windy Day'. This is because he enclosed his landscapes and the subjects of his portraits in circles and triangles placed along diagonal lines. His characteristic manner was to lay thick masses of paint on the canvas, to use a well-planned range of colours and to give sweeping movements to everything that he imagined, rather than copying from nature.

That is what we must love in Soutine; that is what we must understand if we become interested in his creative work.

Those who understand and love his art appreciate the fact that he, who throughout his life learned from the work of other great painters (and was sometimes reproached for it), nevertheless managed to retain his own distinctive style and to paint in his own way; his admiration of other masters was not a loss but a positive gain, thanks to his unfettered imagination. The same may be said of Picasso when he painted dozens of pictures of a small Infanta surrounded by dwarfish figures, after Velazquez's 'Las Meninas' —the artist's imagination is so powerful that he cannot fail to be creative.

It is difficult to imitate Soutine because of the distinctive characteristics which give him a special place among painters. Only de Kooning, in his series of portraits of women and in his landscapes, was fairly successful in approximating Soutine's style of structural composition and his characteristic combinations of greens and blues with reds, but anyone well-acquainted with Soutine's work can easily tell the difference between the two painters. Soutine gives us the profound delight of discovering in his works mysterious wonders of colour and form, which he constructs and reconstructs in his own masterly way to give us a better understanding of his creative aesthetics.

It is a great pity that Soutine, with his outstanding feeling for harmonious and plastic structural design, did not construct more complex compositions, like those of Cézanne. For example, only one of Soutine's portraits, 'Mother and Child', contains two figures. Perhaps this is due to the fact that the Second World War broke out just when he was entering the stage of maturity which would have enabled him to take that course. Soutine was thoroughly depressed by the war, by isolation and by illness. Living in the country, a long way from Paris, he found it difficult to obtain materials; his state of health and his nervous condition, owing to the occupation of France by the Germans, must also have hampered his work.

Soutine's output during his twenty-seven active years was

prodigious. Two years after he arrived in Paris in 1913, his work began to attract attention, but it was not until 1916–1917 that he really began to work well: not 'well' in the way that young artists are supposed to paint when they produce 'good likenesses' of colour and form, but forcefully, not always copying nature but often distorting it—and no one understood why. 'Hey, Soutine, lend me some paint from your pictures. You do slosh it on in layers, don't you?' his colleagues would say, and were told, with a smile, 'I can give you some red if you like, but I'm afraid it will fade—there are no good reds here!'

Soutine's 1915 landscape 'Cité Falguière' is fairly conventional, but in 1917 he painted a portrait of himself at his easel that is a very good likeness, much better than the portrait of him Modigliani did the same year, and very interesting. It shows a feeling which was not apparent in his work three or four years earlier; obviously, his friendship with such artists as Kremègne, Lipschitz, Modi and Rivera had begun to bear fruit. In the same year, under the influence of Courbet, Soutine painted a woman lying in the grass, using a more complex composition than before. (He returned to this subject again in 1934, when he painted it at the country estate of Monsieur and Madame Castaing.)

It will be remembered that Soutine first went to Céret in 1919 and that the style he developed at Céret is quite different from that of the Cagnes Paintings, the atmosphere of the Alpes Maritimes being totally different from that of the Eastern Pyrenees. The Mediterranean landscape is gentler in form and colour and the houses at Cagnes seem to have been built by the hands of individual peasants in different colours, whereas those of Céret form an integral whole with the landscape, both in shape and in colour, fusing with the cliffs, stones and earth to form a wild, turbulent mass which is characteristic of Soutine's 'Céret style'. (However, some of the landscapes he painted at Cagnes, such as 'The Old Mill' in 1922 and 'Cagnes Landscape' the following year, are like abstracts in which the Céret forms are still reflected.)

At first sight, Soutine's Céret landscapes produce an impression of utter chaos. For instance, 'Hills at Céret' (1921) and 'Old

Trees' (1921) seem to constitute an uncoordinated mass of colours, mostly dark; but on closer examination of the thick brush strokes extraordinary, fantastic shapes can be discerned, teeming in the chaotic landscape. All this is painted sharply, energetically, with a certain arrogance; and throughout this period of Soutine's work there runs this feeling of his disturbed wonderment at the Pyrenean landscape, which was so unlike any that the artist had seen before.

It is sometimes said that the Céret paintings are influenced by abstract art, but I believe that the illusion of abstraction is due to foreshortening. Sometimes Nature itself provides subjects for 'abstract art', and the rhythm of Soutine's paintings, especially his landscapes, often depended on the natural structure of his subjects. Thus 'View of the Village' (1921) is painted in zig-zag fashion, to characterize the architectural situation of the village on the uneven, undulating terrain; the foreground is occupied by trees and a seated figure and the background by little houses and hills. Three of the Céret landscapes, painted from a window view, are completely foreshortened. 'Red Roofs' (1921–1922) is viewed from above and the foreshortened houses are seen through the branches of tall trees. 'The Hillock' (1922) and 'The Village Square' are viewed from below. The latter painting seems to be constructed on a plane which to Soutine conformed rhythmically with the structure of the houses and walls surrounding the square; in the left foreground are two reclining figures of peasants taking their rest.

It is important to remember that nearly all the Céret landscapes are constructed diagonally, according to the rules established by El Greco. A mountainous landscape is naturally constructed of diagonals, but the artist must make sure of this himself! All the lines of hill slopes and ravines must run downwards and the hills must be triangular. Soutine used the plan which nature itself had provided and painted on it such secondary subjects as trees, houses and figures. Nature and the artist worked together, but he bent nature to his will, so as to accommodate it more harmoniously into the atmosphere of his painting.

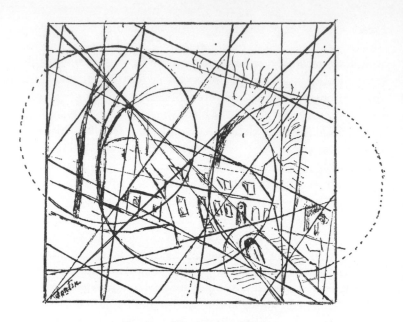

Soutine: The house at Oisème
Reconstruction by Marevna (see fig. 14)

Generally speaking, Soutine's work shows a secrecy in choice of subject and a certain mysteriousness of execution and working methods. Indeed, in some of his works there is evidence of a search for a manner of execution, rather than for a subject. Thus in 'Head of a Woman in Prayer' (1920), probably painted at Céret, the head, a hand and the upper torso form a triangle which seems to serve as a pretext for the portrait. Similarly, in the 'Céret Landscape' (1919) the village houses are sharply inclined from left to right as though they are falling. This is because Soutine constructed the houses, which look rather like cliffs, along diagonal lines. From 1919 onwards, he felt the need to compose his landscapes in such a way that, to the inexpert eye, it seems as though houses, trees, hillocks and roads bend over in different directions, under the influence of some mysterious cataclysm. What such critics as Waldemar George and Paul Guillaume called '*le désordre optique*' was based on soundly constructed plans. After the exhibition of Soutine's work organized by Guillaume in 1927, George wrote, 'All Soutine's work is like a St Vitus dance. All the objects, people and trees whirl about as though drunk, first in one direction and then in the other. The trees and houses spin like tops on the floor'. Later, George reproached Soutine for the general 'unhealthiness' of his work and the distortions in his land-scapes, attributing the latter to the fact that one of Soutine's eyes was weak! It seems strange to me that an eminent art critic should be so 'illiterate' as to fail to understand a painter's aesthetic approach.

I am particularly fond of all Soutine's forest landscapes, of those scampering children, of the colours of the sky after a thunderstorm, with the scattered clouds and the golden gleam of the setting sun glimpsed through the trees. It is because Soutine so loved forests that I have included diagrams of three of his paintings of forests and trees.

The reason for Soutine's predilection is that trees were his first childhood friends, and that he loved them like people. He painted trees with broad, thick brush strokes and scratched marks and curlicues into the foliage with the end of his brush, thus giving the full effect of something really alive and human. The trees whirl as though in a round dance, bowing before the wind, or race along in a bent position, as though running after the children who are hurrying home from school. The most successful picture of this series, based on his childhood memories of Smilovichi, is 'A Windy Day (1929). The reason that the trees seem to race along and sway from side to side is simply that they are painted along diagonal lines: only people who are unaware of the mainsprings of an artist's work will assert that he painted when he was drunk or that his eyesight was defective.

In 1929 Soutine went to Vence, where Chagall now lives. It is a very picturesque village, situated high up among the hills. An enormous old olive tree stands in the village square, the kind of tree about which stories and legends could be woven, and from morning to night the birds rustle about in it, singing, chirping and cooing. Once upon a time there was a bench round the tree on which the old people would shelter from the hot sun. Soutine came to love the old tree and painted two portraits of it, one full face and the other in profile. The huge trunk consists of two thick boughs, entwined and looking like dancing figures. The branches are like so many upraised arms, which seem to be holding up the foliage and the sky above them. A small figure of a man is walking past the bench. A diagram of the second portrait of the tree, in profile, is given here.

The imagery is fantastic: the foliage contains human forms, and Soutine has introduced the face of a monster into the space below the bench. Painting trees always aroused the most extraordinary of his fantasies, bringing the pictures to life and lending them a fairy-tale, childlike atmosphere.

* * *

In 1917 and in 1924, Soutine painted two series of still-lifes with fish. On one canvas of the first series, he depicted a chair on which there is a round plate with four or five fishes. One has protruding, lifelike eyes, which regard you with horror, while the eyes of the others are dead, already receding and glazed. The mouths are exaggeratedly wide open, as though in a scream. The fish are still quivering and seem to be circling round the dish, as if they might leap from it at any moment. There is a curious impression of realism and fantasy intermingled. In this composition Soutine used one central circle—the round plate—flanked by clearly outlined secondary circles, and this gives a remarkable sense of movement to the picture.

Incidentally, I remember once seeing on the table at Soutine's studio a still-life arrangement with a smoked herring on a plate, a dried-up lemon, a knife and a fork—the typical dinner table of the poor artist, which I knew only too well. The arrangement was unappetizing and covered with dust. I mentioned this to Soutine. 'Never mind,' he said, 'if I throw the herring in boiling water, it'll plump up and I can eat it with potatoes and onions.' Perhaps that

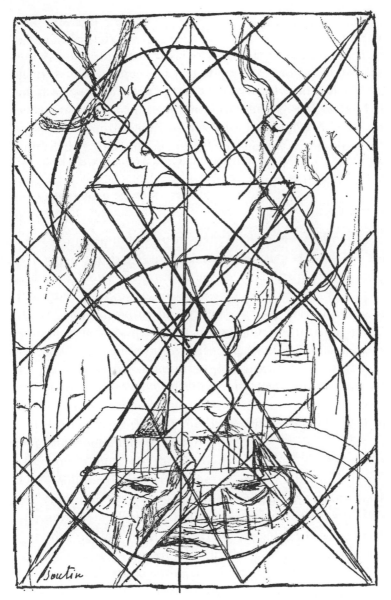

Soutine: The olive tree, small town square, Vence
Reconstruction by Marevna

is exactly what he did do later—I remember during the 1914–1918 war eating dry bread which had been soaked in hot salted water!

In the 1924 series there are two very remarkable still-lifes with skates. The fish form triangles of pink, yellow and mother-of-pearl, and their heads are like the little faces of fantastic, screaming infants. One of the pictures shows a table on which an enormous fish wrapped in paper is lying; on the left hand side are a small jug and a wooden spoon and on the right, a large white bowl with two smoked fish, a lemon and a long French loaf. The composition consists of the large circle containing all the objects in the arrangement; the big skate serves as the basic triangle indispensable to Soutine's compositions. The amazing thing about the picture is that this fish is like a seated creature, half child, half frog (at any rate, half animal), for it seems alive and has arms and legs—a fantastic figment of the artist's imagination. The other still-life with skate is beautiful in colour, but is painted less turbulently, also on the basis of a circle and a triangle. One angle of the fish-triangle reaches to the top of the canvas and, as in the first picture, creates the impression of a swaddled, screaming baby—yet another fantastic image.

Indeed, all Soutine's still-lifes are remarkable not only for their structure, colours and fantastic realism, but for some strange additional quality. There is something unhealthy in Soutine's still-lifes which frightens and disturbs the viewer. The many still-lifes with game by Courbet, under whose influence Soutine painted his, do not arouse this feeling of protest, do not repel one by such a sense of violent death. In 1964, at the remarkable Modigliani-Soutine exhibition at the Tate Gallery in London, an Englishwoman said to me, 'This is all very interesting, but Soutine's still-lifes are terrifying. They give you the same feeling you have when you see a dead body in the street. You want to go closer to see it, but at the same time you're repelled by the smell. You don't know quite what it is lying there—a person, an animal, or a huge bird.'

One picture I remember particularly well at that exhibition is a still-life with a turkey (1926). The huge fowl, half-plucked, is hanging in a Provençal fireplace. It is a fat monster, yellow as

Soutine: Hanging turkey
Reconstruction by Marevna (see fig. 15)

butter, with bluish shadows; the green-black feathers on the neck and head are like locks of hair. The basic colour range of the picture is green-blue, with the yellow carcass of the turkey forming a light, opaque blotch on the dark blue background of the fireplace. The head and the attitude of the body convey a sense of utter tragedy. I cannot forget that fattened, blue-greenish, already rotting carcass. One has the impression that the body of a murder victim has been deliberately arranged in this attitude, that feathers have been stuck on to conceal the body and that the legs have been bent up into a sitting position.

Another still-life with a turkey is similar to the first and no less frightening. The large bird stands out vividly against the dark green background of an old fireplace. On the left hand side of the picture is an expanse of red brick wall, and some tomatoes which have begun to go bad are lying on a napkin on the floor of the fireplace. The body of the great fowl is greenish-yellow, already sunken in places, as though all the fat has been drained out of it; the head is thrown back and a wire fastened to the top of the fireplace is wound round the neck, holding the beak wide open, so that the bird still seems to be uttering its death rattle.

Both these pictures are extremely forceful and rich in colour and they create an indelible impression, as do all Soutine's still-lifes with game. Another, a dead quail lying across a chair, seems to be quivering in its last agony; yet another, showing a pheasant hanging between a window and the mirror of a washstand holding a bowl flanked by apples and a candlestick, is remarkable for its unexpected composition and colouring.

* * *

The evolution of Soutine's portrait painting is most interesting for those who love his work. The self-portrait he painted in 1917 is a presage of the manner in which he was later to convey likenesses despite apparent distortion, and the portraits 'Head of a Man' and 'Man in a Green Jacket,' painted at Céret in 1921, show a slight cubist influence in the angle of the head and body (this did not, however, persist in Soutine's later work).

In 1925 and 1927–1928 he painted a series of portraits of bakers' and butchers' boys, page boys and choir boys in red robes with white surplices. The best known of this series is the 'Page Boy at Maxim's' in his red uniform, painted nearly full-length along diagonal lines reminiscent of El Greco. Indeed, the whole series is based on that master's characteristic structure. To take an interesting subject, whatever it may be, and to find a suitable structure for it is an exercise which has absorbed and attracted painters throughout the ages, and Soutine was no exception. I saw at his studio some old paintings he had bought at the Marché aux puces; he liked to paint over old canvases, in which he discerned ineffable shapes to be adapted to his own style and imagery.

A portrait I find very interesting in construction is the 'Boy in a Round Hat' (1922). When you look at it you are struck by the fact that the big head in the round white hat barely balances on the very thin neck, and the boy looks almost like a puppet whose head is about to fall off. This is entirely due to the structure of the picture: two lines intersect across the canvas and at the point of intersection two angles are formed, a small one containing the head with the hat and a large one containing the body, knees and legs. The intersection point serves the boy as a neck, which Soutine has marked with the little circle of the shirt collar. The boy's profile is drawn in the circle of the head, and this suffices to give the portrait character and to convey a likeness to the model.

Soutine loved to paint children and included their figures in many of his landscapes, but for some reason he produced few children's portraits, although the ones he did paint are full of character and convey something of his own childhood. Thus in 1936 he painted the portrait of a child sitting on a chair sucking his fingers. There is a bed in the background, probably the mother's, and a small chamber pot stands by the chair; the structure is similar to that of Soutine's still-life 'Flowers on a Chair', painted in 1916–1917.

Another late child portrait is the one of a little girl sitting in a field, holding a handkerchief to her face. There is a forest in the

Soutine: The page boy at Maxim
Reconstruction by Marevna

background; we can practically feel the wind, smell the grass and hear the rustle of the trees and the cries of the birds, and yet the girl seems to be sobbing with fear. Is she really crying, or is she simply trying to hide from Soutine, who could be so terrifying when he was working?

A marvellously simple and forceful composition is Soutine's 'Woman in Profile' (1937). This and the superb 'Mother and Child', painted in 1942 shortly before his death, may be regarded as the culmination of his portrait painting.

'Mother and Child' is extremely interesting not only from the point of view of composition but for the strength of its spiritual emotion. Within a structure that is absolutely simple, Soutine has been able to convey something which is usually concealed in his work—a real feeling of humanity. The mother's anxiety for her child is apparent, and I think that this picture originated in Soutine's childhood memories of lying ill on his mother's lap. Certainly this is the painting which most clearly demonstrates his Freudian melancholy about childhood, together with his desire to return to it in spite of himself.

Soutine missed maternal affection all his life. The only human being who bent over him with pity during his unhappy childhood was his mother, and I am sure that she was the only woman for whom he ever had any profound feeling. There was his art, to which he was 'wedded', as he told me, there were models and mistresses who posed for him, but what he really could not do without was friendship. Soutine loved to be surrounded by friends, at work and at leisure, when they drank wine and tea together by the hour, smoking and talking interminably about the art which was their real life.

Epilogue

When Marika was a very young child she was discovered by Isadora Duncan and joined her school. At fourteen she began to earn a living by dancing in ballet, and eventually made enough money to study under the great Preobrajenska. They had many engagements abroad—in Corsica, Switzerland, Holland and a number of large towns in France—and these travels gave her an insight into the life of dancers and their hard-working and disciplined existence. I couldn't go with her most of the time, for I had to work, always painting to sell more canvases and have exhibitions.

We were very short of money, and to add to our finances Marika worked in nightclubs for six months—but she was so exhausted by this that she became very ill. So in 1936 we left Paris for the south of France. We were first in Nice and then in Juan-les-Pines, where Marika met the brother of Serge Lifar. She went to Paris to meet Serge himself; he was impressed with her work and later helped her when she was asked to give a gala performance as a homage to Poland after the German invasion of that country. In 1940 she met Paul Brusset, a talented painter, and married him; the next year they had a little boy. The war was in its second year, and soon after the child was born, Marika and her husband left the baby in the country with a nurse and went to Algiers, hoping to be able to get to England. Unable either to manage this and to join the Allies, she started giving recitals—dance, poetry and mime—for the International Red Cross in Algiers; she also gave independent shows for de Gaulle's *Comité de Libération*. Her husband shared in the great success of her performances, for which he had designed the sets.

From Algiers she went to Tunis and worked and collected money there for the Free French Forces and Liberation Government—she was the only artist doing this work independently, on her own. I stayed in Cannes and was lucky enough to sell a large number of my paintings to an Armenian friend and connoisseur, M. Aseangul of Paris, and the financial benefit from this sale enabled me to take my year-old grandson to live with me in Cannes. An exhibition of my painting was sent over to Algiers to the Galerie de Romanet, but I was not able to go to it myself. In 1945 Marika and her husband returned together to France, but they were divorced shortly afterwards. Marika took a studio for me at Cagnes, and I lived and worked there for two years.

Today the village has a municipal museum, the Château Grimaldi, a twelfth-century edifice that served as a fortress after the Crusades and later as a baronial hall, and some of the rooms in the museum are devoted to modern art. Once or twice a year, there is a great festival with music and dancing, and the people of Cagnes, who so much love to dance, perform a joyous farandole with the artists. On the fourteenth of July, there are fireworks and dancing far into the night. In recent years, many friends of other days are absent, some having become too old for celebrations and others having embarked on that voyage of no return. However, each year the farandole becomes longer and more brilliant, with new artists and a new generation of villagers participating.

While I lived in Cagnes, I talked to many villagers who had vivid recollections of Zborowski's group of artists, especially Modigliani and Soutine, who too soon abandoned the magnificent but perilous path of art and glory. Foremost among the villagers was Monsieur Nicolai, a gross, red-faced man, always short of breath because of a heart condition, who kept a general store where he sold good wine from the regions of St Jeannet and St Paul, cognac and rum. He was the landlord of the studio Modi and Soutine had shared in 1918, and when they left for Paris, still owing him for rent, wine, cognac and meals, Nicolai—all the while sighing and inveighing against art and artists—picked up their discarded canvases and used them to cover his chicken coops and rabbit hutches; good canvas, especially when covered with Soutine's thick layers of paint, provided long-term protection against rain. Years later Nicolai discovered that the pictures of both painters were fetching enormous sums: by 1926, a picture by Modigliani, who had lived on three thousand francs a month in the period between 1918 and 1920, was going for thirty thousand; the prices of Soutine's pictures had also risen. Nicolai rushed to the coops and hutches, where a fortune had been waiting for its hour to come—but alas, all that was left was a mass of rotting canvas.

'My God, Madame Marevna,' Nicolai complained to me, 'who would have thought Soutine would turn out to be a genius? With that face? Forgive me, but really, I have heard that same thing said about others hundreds of times, in every tone of voice. And then, you know, they were always in misery, those two. It's true Monsieur Zborowski sent them money each month—but you know artists! They always get ahead of themselves. They ate the money, always. When it arrived, my wife prepared a feast—ah, for that she's renowned—and made them dishes that would have made Monsieur le Maire himself lick his fingers. They invited all their friends, and they didn't eat, they *devoured*!—word of honour, one would have thought they had never eaten or drunk in their lives!'

Nicolai was not far off the mark: the two painters had eaten too little for too many years.

'You realize that there are always great debts after a dinner like that,' Nicolai went on. 'We ate up money with them—all that wine, all that cognac. And then there was no one to pay. Worse, people laughed at me, saying I was an imbecile. As God is my judge, I grudged them nothing. I gave them all the best. [And the most expensive, I thought, but did not say it.] And the way those two pigs messed up my studio! It's true there was no W.C. But what do you expect? In those days Cagnes was a simple village without conveniences. I gave them a sanitary bucket that they could have emptied somewhere, anywhere. . . . In life, one arranges these little matters. But no, those pigs—geniuses or no geniuses, they were pigs! After they left, my wife and I went one day to take inventory of the broken dishes and we noticed this wall of newspaper packets heaped one on top of another like bricks. And it was solid, you understand. I opened one of the packets and—well—Madame Marevna, it was shit! And so neatly wrapped! Ah, those beasts with their old canvases everywhere, their mountains of cigarette butts! My wife was furious and so was I, by Jove! That's why we took the canvases and put them on the chicken coops and over the rabbit hutches. It's unfortunate, but that's how it was.'

'There's an old proverb that says shit brings good fortune,' I said. 'You should have thrown the packets out of the window and kept the canvases. They were the riches to thank you for your pains and to compensate for the annoyances you suffered. By now you would have been able to build yourself a splendid villa.'

'And I would have a farm—or even two! And a marvellous car! Ah, don't talk about it! Don't say another word about it! I've had good cause to repent. Everybody in Cagnes cursed me, and as for my wife, she practically beat me up. Idiot that I am! But listen to me a little, Madame Marevna. It seems you have talent. I like your portraits of the peasants. I know you're not rich, and I would like to give you credit or buy a canvas from you, but my wife won't allow it. Maybe you or one of these *sans-culottes* here now is a genius. How is one to know? Who thought here that Soutine was a good painter? My poor wife was frightened of him and his pictures when she first saw them. "The devil himself has come to live with us," she said. "His pictures are diabolical—they will bring us bad luck." And now, if anyone were to give me a picture by Soutine, of course I'd hang it up, since he's a recognized genius and his pictures are worth so much, but I'd hang it somewhere in a dark corner. After all, we aren't quite mad yet. But you know, Madame Marevna, we love artists, the devil take them! I sometimes get little presents from the painters here, and my wife invites them to dinner. Ah, she is a very fine cook, my wife,' sighed Nicolai, who had to diet because of his heart.

Poor Nicolai! He died of asphyxia soon after our talk, and I did not have time to give him any presents. Possibly his bad conscience and his regrets hastened his end. All the same, he had some good moments with the artists from Paris: Modigliani, Soutine, and that great wag Kisling (he loved to laugh and joke), who came to Cagnes once in a superb Rolls Royce, with money in his pocket. He just missed breaking his neck on arrival—everyone remembers that. Descending full tilt upon the Place de la Croix, where there were a few huts for road-mending materials against a low parapet overlooking a ravine, Kisling was unable to stop the engine, and the magnificent machine smashed through one of the huts before petrified onlookers, stopping only when its front half was suspended over the ravine. The villagers threw Kisling a rope and all the lads of Cagnes pulled on it together, shouting 'Heave! Heave!' It seemed almost a miracle that they saved both the car and Kisling, who emerged crimson, but beaming with joy—partly because the car was not too badly damaged, partly in anticipation of the celebration to follow.

One person I saw often in Cagnes was the son of Rosalie, the late *patronne* of the famous *crémerie*. He was by then a taciturn middle-aged man, rather untidy but clean, with a closed, expressionless face. He lived alone in a little hut, how I never knew. 'I am a philosopher,' he said of himself. I used to see his silent figure going down to the sea in the mornings and climbing back in the evenings, always alone, like a passing shadow. I wanted to talk to him about the past, but I thought that perhaps it might be painful for him to recollect the time when he had suffered so much from his mother. Was he happy? Did he ever think about that other recipient of his mother's sarcasm and scorn, Modigliani?

While I was in Cagnes I also met Vasilief, whom I had known in Paris in Montparnasse in the canteen he ran during the 1914–1918 war; and Marouchka Diderich, a Russian sculptress whose husband was Austrian and also a sculptor. I visited Matisse in

Nice; he complimented me on my paintings and wrote me a letter about them which was published later in my exhibition catalogues. When I saw him he was already ill and could only walk with sticks. He worked in his bed with gummed coloured paper because he couldn't paint any longer and the results were magnificent.

I paid frequent visits to a house that stood amid shrubbery on a pretty hill. Modi had lived there. I let my gaze wander about the garden, full of shadow and mystery, and imagined him walking or reclining in the shade, reciting verses from *Les Chants de Maldorer* or from Dante.

One day I made a pilgrimage on foot to the nearby village of La Gaude, where Soutine had lived and worked for a time. The sunny road pleased me very much, but the village appeared a little sad, with its grey constructions heaped up one beside the other. It is a small, simple, tranquil family village. The houses are commonplace and most of them have no ornamentation other than the vines clinging to their facades. But their wine cellars, filled with precious bottles, have provisions of joy for all, and the gardens full of flowers smell sweet. Soutine could well have been happy in this peaceful setting. But perhaps he felt alien and melancholy among the villagers, who are of the Italian race and very handsome; they must have reacted with mistrust to this stranger with his Kalmuck face; his red, narrow-lidded, half-closed eyes; his jutting cheekbones; his great thick lips. In the evening, the village must have appeared black and sad after Nice and Paris, with their cafés pulsating with life and gaiety. There is a canvas of Soutine's that depicts the ruined chateau of La Gaude, and I have found his interpretation magnificent: filled with life, mystery and colour. But no one around him at the time understood it. Solitude for Van Gogh, solitude for Soutine, the unloved.

Behind La Gaude are meadows and hills receding towards mountains blue, mauve and finally eternally covered with white, surrounded with azure in summer and in winter enveloped in great clouds that make the Alps appear fairylike, a landscape strange and marvellous. In the evening, when the hills were bathed in shadow, I returned to Cagnes, in the grip of an eerie feeling because I believed I had seen Soutine's face peering out of a window in the house where he had lived.

In 1948, when I had started writing my first book of reminiscences, Marika went to England and I followed her, first to London and then, when she married for the second time, to Dorset, where she went to live with her husband in Athelhampton Hall, a lovely fourteenth-century mansion mentioned in Thomas Hardy's poem, 'The White Lady.' I settled into my own studio, and stayed there for seven years, painting still lifes, landscapes, family portraits, and a large picture of Christ.

Those years in Puddletown in Dorset were very important to me; I grew to know the countryside of England and also English people from the traditional English past—Admiral Charles Turles of Tolpuddle and his family, Lady Angela and Piers Debenham with whom I became firm friends. I shall also never forget how devoted Gerald and Clarice Chinchen, the gardener and his wife at Athelhampton, were to me, nor the delicious fruit pies cooked by Clarice.

When Marika separated from her husband, she thought at first she would stay on in Dorset, but it was too difficult to keep up a big house, and although local friends offered help of all kinds, she finally moved to London with me and her two sons, and we took the house in Ealing which is still our home.

At about this time Professor Robert Herbert of Yale University organised an exhibition of Neo-Impressionists in New York; without knowing who I was, he chose for this exhibition two of my pictures, a nude and a portrait. When, a little later, my first book was published in New York, Professor Herbert saw a copy and decided to seek me out. He came to London and paid me a visit in Ealing. He talked to me of Mr Oscar Ghez and recommended that I get in touch with him, and as a result I had the great good fortune of getting to know this great art collector. He is the Director of the Foundation of Modern Art in Geneva, and arranges magnificent exhibitions in the Petit Palais, where he assembles a great variety of pictures by well-known and lesser-known painters of the Impressionist School and the Ecole de Paris, and makes known to the public the whole range of work belonging to the Belle Epoque. He showed great interest in my work, and in 1971 gave a big retrospective exhibition of it in Geneva.

I am still painting, doing a great many portraits, and I hope one of these days to have an exhibition in London or Paris. When I began painting I found cubism exciting and interesting, and thought that it gave another dimension to painting, since in impressionist art—which preceded cubism—there is little construction. I have followed Cézanne's example—he gave up impressionism on his own and began research into the use of structure by the painters of the Quattrocento, such as Giotto, and his work clearly shows this influence. Structure is of immense importance to me, although I have never altogether abandoned my pointillist style. Diego had been very interested in all that too, and had explained each picture to me. Soutine also was Cézanne's disciple; Diego said that although Soutine had had no artistic education, he understood Cézanne at once, and was his greatest pupil, not only in his use of paint, but in his construction.

Those days in Paris, when we were all together, came back to me vividly when I went to see Ilya Ehrenburg in London in 1960. I visited him three times; each time, upon his arrival in London, he telephoned me in Ealing and gave me just an hour in which to meet him—no more than that. The last time Marika came with me to see him. Ilya read me several pages from his book which was about to be published, and asked my opinion of what he said about Montparnasse and its artists and Rivera and myself. His account made me laugh; it was very childish. He said that Rivera and I were very alike, with the same childlike, enthusiastic and inquisitive character, gay but also violent. Ehrenburg was very afraid of Diego and his Mexican stick, and nicknamed him 'bon anthropophage.' He called me 'fox terrier,' because I ran and jumped and danced, was always playful, and bit my friends on the neck and cheeks. When he heard I was also writing my memoirs he said, 'Marevna, don't be too unkind, don't write too much in black.'

'I don't know what you mean, Ilya,' I replied. 'I write frankly and with all colours, the same way I paint. Not black or rosy or blue, but as I see and feel.'

Ilya also asked me what I thought of the English. Marika and I told him a little about our life and he laughed; he didn't smile often, poor man, for he was already suffering a lot from his heart. But he had not altered a great deal from the old days. The hair framing his face was now white, and this made him look gentler; but the intelligent, ironical gaze and the sceptical smile made me wish to contradict him, as I had done so often in the past. The hour we spent together went all too quickly. I wanted to ask him too many things: about his life, about Soviet Russia, about his last meeting with Rivera. The odd thing is that we talked much of the time about dogs, which he has always loved.

Index

Abstract art, 147, 187
Académie des Beaux Arts,
  balls given by, 32–3
Aesthetics, 172–4
  and see Golden Number; Rivera,
  theories of painting; Soutine,
  structure in his paintings
Aleksinsky, 35, 113
Apollinaire, Guillaume, 18, 182
  and Diego Rivera, 64
  frequenter of the Rotonde, 35
  and Marie Laurencin, 109
  and Max Jacob, 66, 81
  wounded in First World War, 56
Archipenko, 17, 114
Aseangul, M., 200

Bakst, Leon, 51
Balls, *see* Académie des Beaux Arts;
  Russian Academy
Barcelona, 104
Barnes, Dr, 152
Baudeloque Maternity Home, 126–9
Belmont, 35
Beloff, Angelina, 64, 66, 67
  illness and death of her child, 108,
  111–13
  life with Rivera after birth of
  child, 93, 94, 96, 98, 99, 100, 107,
  123–4, 130, 131–2
  pregnancy, 80, 82, 83, 86, 92
  relationship with Diego Rivera,
  73–4, 78, 79, 85, 88–9, 90
Benois, Alexandre, 51
Bergson, Henri, 18, 161
Big Bertha, *see* First World War
Blanchard, Marie, 64, 94
Bonnard, Pierre, 148
Botticelli, 18
Brancusi, 18
Braque, Georges, 35, 138
  at Céret, 146
  and Cubism, 182
  in First World War, 55, 56

Bulakovsky, 17, 18–19
Byzantine art, 174

Cagnes-sur-Mer,
  Marevna's visit to, 203–205
  Musée Grimaldi, 25, 200
  and Soutine's 'Carcass of an Ox',
  166
  Zborowski's artists sent to, 147–9,
  151, 156
Capri, 4, 12
Carmen, 117, 119
Castaing, M., 168, 171, 186
Cendrars, Blaise, 56
Céret, 145-7, 150, 156-7, 186-7
Cerusier, 174
Cézanne, Paul, 143, 183
  and Cubism, 174, 178
  Diego Rivera's admiration for, 64,
  103, 104, 138, 178
  influence on Soutine, 148, 176, 178
  and structure in art, 64, 173, 174,
  178, 179–81, 182, 185
Chagall, Marc, 15, 26, 114, 156, 189;
  plates 6 and 16
Champigny-sur-Veuldre, 171
Chandler, Chapman, 24
Chaplin, Charlie, 35
Cheboksary, 7
Chernoff, 29
Childhood, influence on artists, 6,
  13–15, 26, 143–4
  and see Marevna, childhood of;
  Soutine, childhood of
Chuvash Socialist Republic, 7
Cité Falguière, 17, 186
'Closerie des Lilas', 28
Cocteau, Jean, 18, 54, 81, 179; plate
  5
Colarossi Academy, 28, 57
Construction in painting, *see* Céz-
  anne; Cubism; Rivera, theories
  on painting; Soutine, structure
  in painting of

Cornet, Paul, 66, 71, 72, 117
Courbet, Gustave, 41, 56, 174, 178, 179, 180
    'La forêt aux biches', 41, 56
    influence on Soutine, 42, 143, 144, 170, 179
    'Mademoiselle près de la rivière', 170
    still-lifes with game, 192
Cracow, 20
Craven, Arthur, 25
Cri de Paris, 82
Cubism, 26, 75, 100, 109, 174, 182–3
    linked with Bolshevism, 114
    and Picasso, 66
    Rivera's ideas on, 64, 138, 178, 182–3
    and Soutine, 148, 156–7, 178

Dadaism, 182
Dagusya, 101, 125, 126, 127, 128, 131–2, 134
Dante, 18, 51, 61, 204
Delevsky, 59–60, 61, 62, 113
Delhaye, André, 35, 117
Diaghilev, Serge, 95; plate 5
    Diaghilev Ballet, 51–2
Diderich, Marouchka, 203
Dôme, café, 25, 100, 117, 171
Drawing, 17, 21, 145, 159
Drugs, 116, 147, 149

Ecole des Beaux Arts, 21
Ehrenburg, Ilya, 29, 37–8, 39, 58, 71, 80, 117, 118; plate 6
    appearance of, 37, 50, 51
    at Eze, 74-7, 90
    friend of Rivera, 66, 79, 82, 84–85, 86, 89, 104, 109
    ill health of, 72–3
    meeting with Marevna in London, 1960, 206–207
    returns to Russia, 113
    at the Rotonde, 35, 45, 46, 49
    visit to Picasso, 67
    war correspondent, 55
    work at Paris station, 56–7, 171
Ehrenburg, Katya, 37, 45, 67, 71, 76–7, 90, 113, 117
Ensor, 26, 177
Estonia, 27

Expressionism, 20, 26, 147, 177, 178
Eze, 74–7, 90

Faure, Dr Elie, 150, 153, 156, 181
Fauvism, 26, 178
Favory, 35, 55, 56
Fénéon, Felix, 110
Finland, 27
First World War, 24–5, 26, 55–6, 108–109, 192
    armistice, 119–20
    bombardment of Paris by Big Bertha, 116
    and effect of Russian Revolution, 114–16
Fishers, friends of Rivera, 105–106, 123, 132, 137, 138–9; plate 8
Flemish art, 103
Florence, 18
Foreign Legion, 24, 55
Foujito, 33
Friesz, 64, 66
Futurism, 64

Gaude, La, 204
Gausset, surgeon, 172
George, Waldemar, 20, 188–9
Georgia, 10, 11
Ghez, Oscar, 205
Giotto, 18, 103, 173–4, 178, 179, 180, 182
Gleize, 182
Gogol, N., 11
Golden Number, the, 174
Golden Section, diagram of, 176
Gontcharova, 35, 51, 64; plate 5
Gorki, Maxim, 12, 24, 89, 102
Gorki, Yura, 12, 77, 96, 99, 102, 109
Gottlieb, 21
Goya, F., 37, 138
Greco, El, 66, 103, 138, 183, 187, 195
Greece, 174
Grimm, 172
Gris, Juan, 35, 64, 138, 174
Guillaume, Paul, 18, 152–3, 188–9

Hastings, Beatrice, 117–19
Hébuterne, Jeanne, 149
Herbert, Robert L., 205
Hödler, 177
Hollywood, 25

Impressionism, 110, 178, 179
Ingres, J. A. D., 106
Israel, 26
Italian art, 18, 148, 173–4, 179
Italy, 174

Jacob, Max, 18, 35, 64, 66, 68–9, 80, 81
  Ars poétique, 68
  at Céret, 145–6
  death of, 171
  dissoluteness of, 69, 117–19, 147
  and Picasso, 50, 51, 69, 148
  Poèmes en prose, 68
Japan, and Japanese art, 26

Kahn, Gustave, ix, 58
Kandinsky, 35
Katz, Mané, 25–7; plates 3 and 4
Kazan District, 7, 40
Kazanka, river, 7
Kharkov Fine Arts Academy, 26
Kiev, 27, 37, 184
Kikoine, Misha, 25, 35, 57, 172; plate 1
  education and early relations with Soutine, 16, 17
  expressionist influence on, 177
  at La Ruche, 19, 20
  patronized by Zborowski, 22
Kisling, Moïse, 20–2, 23, 24–5, 66, 69; plate 2
  in Cagnes, 148, 203
  death of, 25
  joins Foreign Legion 24, 55
  and the Rotonde, 33, 35
  and Zborowski, 145
Kokoschka, O., 26, 177
Koltsov, 11
Kooning, Wilhelm de, 185
Kremègne, Pinchus, 22, 25, 29, 35, 57, 58, 172, 186
  at Céret, 146
  early education and friendship with Soutine, 16–17, 19, 20
  expressionist influence on, 177
  at the Rotonde, 33, 35
Kremenchuf, 25
Kremlin, 3
Kropotkin, N., *Memoirs of a Revolutionary*, 18
Kruger, 16

Lagny-sur-Marne, 123
Larionov, 35, 51, 64; plate 5
Laurencin, Marie, 25, 83, 109
Lautréamont, 18, 61
Leblanc, patron of the Rotonde, 33, 46, 56, 57
Léger, Fernand, 35, 55, 56, 66, 69; plate 6
Léger, Jeanne, 69–73
Lenin, V. I., 35
Leonardo da Vinci, 173, 174, 178
Lermontov, M. Y., 11
Lhote, André, 35, 55, 64, 95
Lifar, Serge, 199
Lipschitz, 17, 64, 186
Lisbon, 25
Loeb, Pierre, 153
London, 161, 205
Louvre, the, 41, 43, 56, 83, 177
Lunacharsky, 29, 113

Madrid, 104
Marevna, 50; plates, 2, 4, 5, 6, 7, 9, 10 and 12
  childhood of, 6–11
  begins relationship with Diego Rivera, 63–6, 73–4, 77–80, 82–3, 84–93
  convalescence at Èze, 74–7
  copies Courbet's 'La forêt aux biches', 41–2, 44–5, 56
  difficulties of relationship with Rivera, 110–11
  in Dorset, England, 205
  education of, 11–12
  end of relationship with Rivera, 129–39
  experiences anti-Russian feeling in Paris, 115–16
  experiments with alcohol and drugs, 116–19
  falls ill in Montparnasse room taken by Rivera, 100–102
  and father's death, 43–5, 47–9, 68
  in hospital in Paris and birth of Marika, 126–9
  illness after a fall, 70–3
  at Lagny-sur-Marne, 123–5
  lives with Rivera in his studio, 93–9
  lying in at Châtillon, 125–6

meeting with Ehrenburg in London, 1960, 206–207
and name 'Marevna', 12, 22–3
relationship with Soutine, 143, 153–66
relationship with Zadkine, 35–7
return to Paris on outbreak of war, conditions, 56–8
at Russian Academy balls, 29, 31–2
tries to have baby by Rivera, 120–2
visits Cagnes and works there, 200–205
Marika, ix, 132, 133, 137, 153, 157, 199–200; plate 10
birth of, 128–30
meetings with Soutine, 154–5, 157, 158
relationship with father, 134, 135–6
Markov, 35, 113
Massine, Leonide, 80
Matisse, Henri, 26, 35, 64, 66, 82, 95, 182
Mazas, Pierre, 26–7
Mechnikov, 102
Meshchaninov, Oscar, 64, 77, 160–1
Mestranovic, Oscar, 17
Metzinger, 35, 55, 56, 182
Mexico, 95, 103–105, 134, 136, 137, 138
Ministère des Beaux Arts, 55
Minkevich, M., 41, 44–6
Minsk, 12, 16, 27, 159
Mishka, 9
Mitrani, 117, 119
Modigliani, Amedeo, 23, 33, 35, 55, 57, 64, 66, 118, 156
appearance of, 50, 51, 61
at Cagnes, 200–202
death of, 148–9, 172
and drawing, 145, 159
dissipation of, 21, 59, 61–2, 63, 69, 117–19, 147, 149
and friendship with Soutine, 17-18, 20, 149, 186, 192
patronized by Zborowski, 21, 22, 148–49, 200, 201
at Russian Academy in Paris, 27
Monet, Claude, 179
Montparnasse, 20–2, 26, 27, 33, 35,

59, 62, 66, 67, 70, 82, 116, 148, 149, 171, 172
Moscow, 3, 5, 11, 27
Mouat, Dagmar, 27
Moulin de la Galette, 28
Munch, Edvard, 26, 177

Naples, 18, 62
Negro art, 60, 66
'New Art', the, 178, 179
New York, 25, 26
Nicolai, M., 200–203
Nietzsche, F., 18
Nyanyushka, 7

Odessa, 27
Olivier, Dr, 172
Orloff, Chana, 27
Orlova, 114
Ortiz, 33

Parade, 52
Petrov, 157
Picabia, 35
Picasso, Pablo, 18, 35, 56, 66–7, 83; plates 5 and 6
appearance of, 50, 51, 66–7, 78
at Céret, 145–6
and Cubism, 174, 182, 183
and designs for Parade, 52
and Diego Rivera, 64, 95, 97, 104, 138
friendship with Max Jacob, 66, 69, 148
and Velazquez's 'Las Meninas', 185
Pinard, Professor, 120–1, 127
Pissaro, Camille, 179
Pite, Madame, 125, 130, 131, 133
Pointillism, 109–10, 156, 179, 184
Poiret's, 66
Poland, 20, 21, 27
Pompeii, frescoes of, 174, 178
Poussin, C., 174, 178
Provence, 179, 181; plate 9
Pushkin, A., 11

Quotidien, Le, 58

Ravenna, 184
Rayonnistes, 183
Rembrandt, 166, 168, 179
Renaissance painting, 173, 174, 179

Renoir, Auguste, 147, 176
Repin, 184
Riga, 27
Rivera, Diego, ix, 18, 35, 50, 51, 65, 71, 118, 159, 206; plates 6 and 8
  attitude to Marevna after Marika's birth, 129–32, 134–6
  declares his love for Marevna, 84–93
  drawings, 106–107, 135
  early relationship with Marevna, 64–6, 73–4, 77, 78–83
  fits of 'lunacy', 78, 97, 124
  happiness in his relationship with Marevna, 103–109, 121–2, 123–4
  hires room for Marevna in Montparnasse, 100–102
  illness and death of son, 108, 111–13
  life in Mexico, 104–105
  lives with Marevna at his studio, 93–9
  and Madame S., 58, 94, 96, 98, 99
  return to Mexico, 134–5, 136–7
  and Soutine, 64, 150, 153, 186
  and theories of painting, 64, 95, 103, 138, 157, 174, 176, 178, 182–3
  'La Vierge enceinte', 73
  weakness of character and relationship with Marevna, 110–11, 125, 126, 132, 138
  see also Beloff, Angelina
Rivière, Marcel, 82
Rome, 3, 5, 11, 18
Rosalie's crémerie, 62–3, 66, 105, 108–109, 203
Rosenberg, Paul, 82–3, 86, 87, 138
Rosenblum, Vitya, 117–19
Rotonde, café, 25, 66, 71, 100, 113, 159
  centre of artistic life and meeting place, 33–5, 49, 56–7, 62, 171
  and Ehrenburg, 38, 49, 73
  Minkevich affair, 41, 45–6
  Modigliani's expulsion from, 117
Rousseau, le douanier, 104, 138
Rubinstein, Artur, 25
Ruche, La, 17, 18, 19
Russia, 6–11, 12–17, 26
  1917 Revolution, 113–15
Russians in Paris, 4, 5, 17–20, 25–6
  canteens, 59–62

charity balls sponsored by, 28–30, 31–2
at the Rotonde, 35
Russian Academy, 18, 27–8

S., M. and Mme., patrons of the Arts, 58, 80, 94, 96, 98, 99, 105
  and see Rivera, and Mme. S.
Sacre du Printemps, Le, 52
St Peter's, 3
St Petersburg, 27, 59
Sakharova, Olga, 27
Salle Bullier, 28
Salle Drouot, 166
Salon d'Automne, 126
Salon des Independents, 73
San Carlos Fine Arts Academy, 104
Santé prison, 5–6, 36–7
Satie, Eric, 18
Saugrade, 35, 55, 156
Savinkov, Boris, 35, 39–40, 66, 129
  appearance of, 40
  friendship with Marevna, 39–40, 82, 109, 122, 127, 129
  at house of Mme. S., 58, 80
  marriage, 76
  The Pale Horse, 40
  visits Picasso, 67
  war correspondent, 55
Savinkov, Marusaya, 76, 120, 122
Sazonov, 59
Schoenberg, David, 113–14
Second World War, 25, 171, 185
Seurat, Georges, 110, 174
Signac, 110
Sisley, Alfred, 179
Smilovichi, 12, 144, 159, 161, 189
Soutine, Chaim, 6, 14, 23, 25, 29, 50, 51, 59, 60, 64, 94, 114, 119; plate 12
  affinities with Vrubel, 183–4
  arrival in Paris, 17–18, 178
  art education of, 16–17, 177, 178
  at Cagnes-sur-Mer, 147–9, 151, 156, 186, 200–203
  at Céret, 145–7, 150, 156–7, 186–7, 188
  and Cézanne, 143, 148, 176, 178
  childhood of, 12–16, 143–4, 159, 173, 189, 197
  and Courbet, 42, 143, 179, 186, 192

death of, 171–2
and drawing, 17, 145, 159
exhibition arranged by Guillaume, 1927, 152–3, 189
friendship with Marevna, 57–8, 153–166
friendship with Modigliani, 17–18, 20, 62, 63, 148–9, 186
ill health of, 17, 55, 149–50, 154, 160, 171, 172
landscape painting of, 143, 144–5, 147, 148, 153, 156–7, 158, 184, 186–7, 188–90
paintings by:
 'Boy in a Round Hat', 195
 'Cagnes Landscape', 186
 'Carcass of an Ox', 166–8; plate 11
 'Céret Landscape', 188
 'Cité Falguière', 186
 'Flowers on a Chair', 195
 'Hanging Turkey', 192–4; plate 15
 'Head of a Man', 194
 'Head of a Woman in Prayer', 188
 'The Hillock', 187
 'Hills at Céret', 186–7
 'House at Oisème', 188; plate 14
 'Man in a Green Jacket', 194
 'Mother and Child', 171, 185, 197
 'The Old Hill', 186
 'Old Trees', 186–7
 'Page Boy at Maxim's', 195, 196
 'Red Roofs', 187
 'View of the Village', 187
 'The Village Square', 187
 'A Windy Day', 184, 189; plate 13
 'Woman bathing', 168, 169; plate 13
 'Woman in profile', 197
 'Woman lying in the grass', 168–70
patronized by Zborowski, 18, 21, 22, 145–8, 150–2, 153, 199, 200, 201
portraits, 158, 159, 185, 188, 190, 194–7
quality of paints used by, 170–1, 186

relationship with his father, 13, 15, 164–6
at the Rotonde, 33, 35
at La Ruche, 19-20
at the Russian Academy in Paris, 27–8
social consequences of growing fame, 160–4
still-lifes, 166–8, 190, 192–4, 195
structure in his pictures, 148, 173, 176, 178, 181, 183, 184–5, 187–90, 195, 197
Tate Gallery exhibition, 192
at Vence, 189–90, 191
his views on art, 176–8, 182–3
works for Dr Barnes, 152
Spain, 25, 104
Stebelsky, Bronislav Vikientievish, father of Marevna, 7–11
 death, and its effect on Marevna, 43–5, 47–9, 68
Stein, Leo, 66
Stravinsky, Igor, plate 5
Stroganov School, Moscow, 11

Tartars, 7
Tate Gallery, 192
Tiflis, 5, 10, 27, 44, 75, 101
Tikhon, 74, 76–7, 113
Tintoretto, 18, 179
Titian, 179
Toledo, 104
Toloiga, 104
Tordello, 184
Tretyakosky Gallery, 184
Trotsky, Leon, 35
Turgenev Library, Paris, 59

United States of America, 25, 172
Utrillo, 57

Valadon, 57
Van Gogh, Vincent, 20, 144, 148, 177–8, 181, 204
Vasilief, 203
Vassilieva, Marie, 35, 60–1, 114
Velazquez, 138, 185
Venice, 18, 184
Verlaine, Paul, 18
Vilna, 16
 Fine Arts Academy of, 16–17, 20

Vitebsk, 27
Vitruvius, 174
Volga, 6
Voloshin, Max, 35, 66, 77, 113
    appearance and character, 38–9, 50,
        51
    friendship with Marevna, 38–9,
        71–2, 81–2, 83, 89, 102, 109
    at Mme. S.'s, 58, 80
    visit to Picasso, 67
Vrubel, 183–4

Warsaw, 41
Wilde, Oscar, 18

Zadkine, Ossip, 17, 40, 48–9, 66, 114,
    161
    appearance and character, 27–8
    and 'The Camel's Tango', 61
    friendship with Marevna, 35–7
    joins Foreign Legion, 55
Zamaron, Léon, 57, 157
Zarette, Ortiz de, 21
Zborowski, patron of Soutine and
    Modigliani, 18, 21, 145–8, 150–2,
    153, 200, 201
    and Kisling, 22
    and Marevna, 22, 156